Irish Puddings, Tarts, Crumbles, and Fools

for three great cooks:

my grandmother, Minnie Sullivan Barry;

my mother, Catherine Barry McGlew;

and my daughter, Catherine Barry Johnson

Irish Puddings, Tarts, Crumbles, and Fools

80 GLORIOUS DESSERTS

by **MARGARET M. JOHNSON**

photographs by **MARGARET M. JOHNSON**
food photographs by **LEIGH BEISCH**

CHRONICLE BOOKS
SAN FRANCISCO

ACKNOWLEDGMENTS

I'd like to express my thanks to the chefs, hoteliers, restaurateurs, and Irish home cooks who contributed recipes and advice for this book, especially to members of the Hidden Ireland, a collection of private homes that are open to guests, and my friend Noel McMeel, head chef at Castle Leslie, Glaslough, County Monaghan. Thanks to Bord Bia (Irish Food Board) in Dublin and Chicago, for their inspiration and assistance; Orla Carey and Tourism Ireland, New York, for travel and promotional support; Roisin Hennerty and Molly O'Loughlin, Irish Dairy Board, Chicago, for product donations; Flahavans, Odlums, and McCann's Irish oatmeal companies for oatmeal history and recipes; Barry's, Bewley's, and Lyons Tea companies for tea history and brewing tips; Brian Nolan for Celtic traditions and tidbits; Steve MacDonagh, Brandon Publishers, for editorial assistance with "Wren Day" traditions; Chef John Murphy and his Culinary Arts students at Barry Tech, Westbury, N.Y., for assistance with recipe testing; Teisha Covino for assistance with recipe testing; Madeleine Morel, my agent, who continues to provide guidance and encouragement; Bill LeBlond, editorial director, cookbooks, Chronicle Books, for his faith in me again; Amy Treadwell and Holly Burrows, Chronicle Books, for their editorial assistance; and my husband, Carl, for his indulgence in all things Irish!

The recipes for Tipsy Pudding in Spiced Wine with Honey Cream Cheese (page 23), Irish Coffee Crèmes Caramels with Irish Coffee Sauce (page 35), Gooseberry-Mead Swiss Roll (page 119), and Posset Cúchulainn (page 94) are adapted with the permission of Bord Bia (Irish Food Board). The recipe for Plum Tart with Oatmeal Crust (page 59) is reproduced with permission of the Oat Millers of Ireland.

The Jenny Bristow quote from *Highdays & Holidays* (1991), page 13, is reprinted by permission of Gill and Macmillan Ltd., Dublin, Ireland, and Ulster Television. The Monica Sheridan quote from *The Art of Irish Cooking* (1965), page 99, is reprinted by permission of Hippocrene Books, New York. The Alice Taylor quotes from *The Night Before Christmas* (1994), pages 139 and 152, and the Steve MacDonogh quote from *Green and Gold: The Wrenboys of Dingle* (1983), page 161, are reprinted by permission of Brandon Publishers, Dingle, Ireland.

Page 2: Rainbow over Delphi Mountains, County Galway
Page 66: Photo courtesy of Odlums Oatmeal Company
Page 161: Photo courtesy of Bernie Coogin

Library of Congress Cataloging-in-Publication
Data available.

ISBN 0-8118-4163-4

Manufactured in Singapore

Design by Brett MacFadden
Prop styling by Sara Slavin
Food styling by Dan Becker
Typesetting by Kristen Wurz
Set in Neutra, AT Sackers, and Apollo MT

Distributed in Canada by Raincoast Books
9050 Shaughnessy Street
Vancouver, British Columbia V6P 6E5

10 9 8 7 6 5 4 3 2 1

Chronicle Books LLC
85 Second Street
San Francisco, California 94105
www.chroniclebooks.com

TABLE OF CONTENTS

INTRODUCTION

"Life is uncertain: eat dessert first."

—SOL GORDON AND HAROLD BRECHER

I am not my mother's daughter when it comes to sweets. She was one of the best bakers and dessert makers I've ever known, but, regrettably, she did not pass the baker's gene on to me. For most of my childhood, she was a stay-at-home mom, so when we arrived home after school the house was usually filled with the aroma of something wonderful she had just taken out of the oven. Like June Cleaver or Harriet Nelson, she had some kind of homemade cookie, pie, or cake sitting on a rack in the middle of the kitchen table. She always said she inherited her kitchen skills from her Irish mother, Minnie Sullivan, who emigrated from Rathmore, County Kerry, to Boston around 1900.

My mother kept loads of hand-written recipes on butter-stained and vanilla-spotted pages in a dilapidated book with a torn green cover. She had many more, also hand-written, on index cards she gathered from "recipe swaps" sponsored by the Daughters of Isabella, a church-affiliated woman's club to which she belonged. Among these were Edna Finnegan's Confections for a Candy Tray, Yvonne Lucey's Banana Tea Bread, Mary O'Brien's Peanut Blossoms, and Ann Cronin's Apple Tart.

She kept hundreds more neatly clipped from the "Confidential Chat" section of the *Boston Globe*. After she died, my sister and I found the tattered brown box—an old yeast container marked Cobb, Bates & Yerxa Co., Established 1871, Boston, Taunton, Fall River—where she kept some of her mother's recipes along with her snippets from the "Chat": Bread Pudding Delight, Hot Milk Sponge Cake, Large Cocoa Cake, Whole Wheat Bread, Date and Fig Bars, Good Plain Cake, Icebox Rolls, War Cake, Surprise Cream Cake, Excellent Dark Cake, Prized Pineapple Pie, Rhubarb Fool, Congo Bars, and Hermits.

The dog-eared recipe for Genuine Irish Soda Bread, subtitled "A reprint from Maura Laverty who radiocasts in Eire," made its annual appearance around

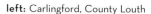

curd, thick-cut orange marmalade, and clotted cream, which I shamelessly spread on soda bread at breakfast and on scones later at afternoon tea. I learned that most sweets fall under the generic name of "pudding," so regardless of whether I was offered a lemon sponge, a chocolate fondant, or a strawberry fool, it arrived as my "pud." I indulged with abandon and was determined to change my ways.

On visit after visit, I began to coax recipes out of shop owners, bakers, and chefs—people like Christina Ryan of the Cafe on the Quay, in Kinvara, County Galway, who unfloured her hands just long enough to jot down her scone recipe; or Peter Kellett, proprietor of the Baker's Oven in Kinsale, County Cork, whom I persuaded to divulge his recipe for brown soda bread with sesame seeds, although he had sworn the recipe would never leave his shop; or Meryl Long, hostess of Martinstown House, County Kildare, who gave me not only her recipe for orange sponge cake, but also a delightful story about its origin at tennis parties. On most occasions, the request was a measure of applause for the baker or chef, a private award given by a visiting American who would publish that recipe and acknowledge its goodness.

The recipes in *Irish Puddings, Tarts, Crumbles, and Fools* not only acknowledge baked goods and desserts as integral parts of an Irish meal, but also serve as sweet reminders of Ireland and the ever-improving state of its cuisine. But while many of the recipes were generously provided by pastry chefs working there, they are not restaurant recipes in the professional sense, although suggestions for individual restaurant-size servings are provided. There are no recipes for spun-sugar towers meant to emerge from exotic sorbets;

St. Patrick's Day. The fact that it was reprinted from a 1946 issue of *Vogue* magazine was boldly underlined, adding, I guess, even more significance. At one time or another, my mother tried them all, and we were the lucky beneficiaries. When she told us to "save room for dessert," we took notice.

Unlike my mother, I worked outside the house, so except for special occasions like birthdays and dinner parties, slice-and-bake cookies, cake mixes, and ready-to-bake pie crusts were the genesis of most desserts in my house; that is, until I went to Ireland and discovered my lost baking heritage.

There I found ordinary women who would rise at the crack of dawn to bake soda breads, biscuits, and scones to serve their B&B guests at breakfast. In Kildare, Monaghan, and Donegal, I discovered lemon

none for complicated caramel-coated cream puffs or mile-high layers of puff pastry cuddling crème pâtissière. There are no instructions for creating whimsical chocolate-covered ants designed to dance across plates, and with the exception of a few Christmas cakes for which you need to soak fruit overnight to plump it up a bit, there are none that require many hours of preparation before the dish can be assembled.

Instead, the recipes in these pages are contemporary renditions of traditional Irish desserts—puddings, tarts, crumbles, crisps, cakes, flummeries, and fools—dishes that a Dublin pastry chef aptly described as "high-end comfort food." And because no discussion of Irish sweets would be complete without recipes for Christmas—the most important holiday on the Irish baking calendar—and for "tea"—both the simple evening meal of cold meats, breads, and sweets, and the more formal ceremony known as "high tea"—*Irish Puddings, Tarts, Crumbles, and Fools* includes additional chapters devoted exclusively to Christmas sweets and to breads and cakes for tea.

Since the very earliest times, fruit has been sweetened with honey and stewed to make puddings, pastries, and cakes for dessert, perhaps the most universally loved of all dishes. Desserts represent the best of a culture and a cuisine, and Irish desserts are no exception. Cookery writer Theodora FitzGibbon once said: "All Irish people have a very sweet tooth and will spend hours making elaborate puddings and decorating cakes for the delectation of themselves and their families." In *Irish Puddings, Tarts, Crumbles, and Fools,* you'll find more than eighty delicious recipes to help further this tradition.

Bain taitneamh as do bhéile! Bon appétit.

Ballyvaughan, County Clare

puddings

Ulster cook Jenny Bristow once said that "to arrive at pudding time is to arrive at the best part of the meal. Puddings, desserts, sweets—call them what you will—be they boiled, steamed, or baked, will always be to me honest, down-to-earth ideas flavored not only with sauces but a little nostalgia."

Historically, puddings were often made with wild fruits—raspberries, cherries, blackberries, strawberries, bilberries, and sloes, a plumlike fruit—sweetened with honey, thickened with suet, carrageen, or fresh cream, and slowly stewed over the fire. Bearing names like almond cream, apple amber, barley flummery, bilberry mousse, lemon pudding, black currant sponge, baked custard, or honeycomb mould, all of these traditional soft, creamy, custardy dishes answered to the name of "pudding."

Probably the most widely known is bread pudding, which was first noted in culinary history in the late 1600s. The pudding was originally invented as a way of using up stale bread and is a simple combination of bread, milk, eggs, and sugar, although dried fruits, especially raisins or currants, are often added along with spices like nutmeg and cinnamon. Rice pudding is also a simple concoction, as are any number of traditional fruit-based puddings that come with delicate sponge toppings. Today's puddings are more elaborate affairs—velvety crèmes brûlees, ethereal soufflés, and crunchy bavarois to name a few—and they provide even more reasons to "save room for dessert."

Bread and Butter Pudding

Bread pudding, a classic Irish sweet, is also called bread and butter pudding when the slices of bread are buttered first, a touch that adds a richer flavor. When raisins or golden raisins are added, they are often plumped up first with a few hours' soaking in Irish whiskey. Contemporary versions might include fruits such as apples, blueberries, pears, rhubarb, and dried cranberries, or dark or white chocolate pieces (see the variations on page 16). This recipe is the most traditional, adapted from ones you'll find throughout Ireland, including at the Lime Tree in Kenmare, County Kerry; Aherne's in Youghal, County Cork; and Ballynahinch Castle, in Recess, County Galway. For restaurant service, chefs make the puddings in 6- or 8-ounce ramekins, or even teacups, but you can bake the pudding family style in a 9-inch baking dish, as suggested in this recipe. Custard Sauce (page 16) is a favorite traditional accompaniment, although Irish Whiskey Sauce is also popular (page 16). Sauces should be made first and chilled before serving. **Serves 6 to 8**

½ cup raisins

½ cup Irish whiskey

5 large eggs

2 cups heavy (whipping) cream

1 cup sugar

½ teaspoon ground cinnamon

¼ teaspoon ground nutmeg

Vanilla bean (see Note) or
1 teaspoon vanilla extract

8 ounces (8 to 9 slices) firm white bread, crust left on

4 tablespoons unsalted Kerrygold Irish butter, at room temperature

Custard Sauce or Irish Whiskey Sauce (optional, page 16)

In a small bowl, combine the raisins and whiskey and let soak for 1 hour. Butter a 9-inch square glass baking dish.

In a large bowl, whisk together the eggs, cream, sugar, cinnamon, and nutmeg. Split the vanilla bean in half lengthwise and scrape out the seeds and drop them into the custard, or add the vanilla extract.

Spread one side of each slice of bread with butter. Cut the slices in half diagonally and arrange half the bread, overlapping the slices, in the bottom of the baking dish. Drain the raisins and sprinkle half over the bread. Repeat with remaining bread and raisins. Pour the custard over the bread and let soak for 30 minutes.

Preheat the oven to 400°F. Place the baking dish in a large baking pan. Add enough hot water to come halfway up the sides of the dish. Bake for 50 to 60 minutes, or until the pudding is set and the top is golden. Remove the baking dish from the water and let cool on a wire rack. Serve warm with a chilled sauce, if desired.

NOTE: Vanilla beans, which are actually seed pods, can be found in the baking or spices section of most supermarkets. For maximum flavor, slice the pod down its length and scrape the point of the knife along the inside to release the seeds. Vanilla pods are quite expensive (as much as 7 dollars for two pods), but the flavor is worth it. After the seeds are scraped out, you can make vanilla

(continued)

Bread and Butter Pudding *(continued)*

sugar by putting the pods into a lidded jar of superfine sugar. Use the sugar in cakes, sauces, and other desserts. You can continue to add used pods and replace with more sugar as needed.

Variations

Chocolate Bread Pudding: Omit the raisins and whiskey. Substitute 1 cup of semisweet chocolate chips and ½ cup of white chocolate chips.

Harvest Bread Pudding: Omit the raisins and whiskey. Substitute 1 apple, peeled, cored, and cut into ½-inch pieces and ½ cup dried cranberries.

Strawberry Bread Pudding: Omit the raisins and whiskey. Substitute ¾ cup of sliced fresh strawberries.

Rhubarb Bread Pudding: At Kilmokea Manor, Great Island, in County Wexford, Emma Hewlitt makes rhubarb bread puddings in individual glass custard cups, which show off the color of the fruit. Omit the raisins and whiskey. Chop 8 stalks of rhubarb into small pieces. Cut 12 slices of bread into 3-inch rounds. Layer the fruit in between 3 rounds of bread in each of eight 6-ounce glass custard cups. Whisk together the eggs, cream, sugar, and spices and add the vanilla. Spoon the mixture into the custard cups and bake for 40 to 45 minutes. **Serves 8**

Blueberry Bread Pudding: At Ghan House, in Carlingford, in County Louth, chef Chris Diggins makes bread pudding with toasted croissants and blueberries. Omit the raisins, whiskey, and bread. Cut 8 croissants into 2-inch pieces and toast them in a 375°F oven for 10 minutes. Combine the toasted croissant pieces with 2 cups of fresh blueberries in the baking dish. Whisk together the eggs, cream, sugar, and spices, and add the vanilla. Spoon over the croissants. Sprinkle with 2 tablespoons of slivered almonds, and bake as above. Serve with Lemon Curd (page 134) or Lemon Curd Cream (page 107). **Serves 6 to 8**

Custard Sauce:

¾ cup milk

¾ cup heavy (whipping) cream

½ vanilla bean, split lengthwise

5 large egg yolks

½ cup sugar

In a medium saucepan over medium heat, combine the milk, cream, and vanilla. Bring to a boil, stirring constantly, then reduce heat to simmer. In a small bowl, whisk together the egg yolks and sugar. Stir into the cream mixture and cook, stirring frequently, for 8 to 10 minutes, or until the mixture thickens and coats the back of a spoon. Strain into a small bowl. Cover and refrigerate for 1 hour, or until chilled. Can be refrigerated for up to 24 hours. **Makes about 1½ cups**

Irish Whiskey Sauce:

¾ cup heavy (whipping) cream

⅓ cup Irish whiskey

¼ cup sugar

½ teaspoon vanilla extract

1 tablespoon water

¼ teaspoon cornstarch

In a small saucepan over medium heat, combine the cream, whiskey, sugar, and vanilla. Bring to a boil, stirring constantly, then reduce heat to simmer. Mix the water and cornstarch in a small bowl until smooth. Add to the cream mixture. Simmer for 8 to 10 minutes, or until the sauce thickens and coats the back of a spoon. Transfer to a small bowl, cover, and refrigerate for 1 hour, or until chilled. Can be refrigerated for up to 24 hours. **Makes about 1 cup**

Lemon and Almond Pudding with Blueberry Sauce

This recipe for an old-fashioned lemon pudding results in a two-layer affair of rich custard on the bottom and a spongelike cake on top. It's often served with Blueberry Sauce, or commercially made blueberry coulis from Derryvilla Farm (see page 95). **Serves 6**

PUDDING

¼ cup all-purpose flour

1 cup sugar

4 tablespoons unsalted Kerrygold Irish butter, melted

Scant ½ cup fresh lemon juice

1 tablespoon grated lemon zest

½ teaspoon almond extract

3 large eggs, separated

1½ cups buttermilk

BLUEBERRY SAUCE

2 cups fresh blueberries

½ cup water

¼ cup sugar

1 teaspoon fresh lemon juice

2 teaspoons cornstarch

Preheat the oven to 325°F. Butter a 9 x 5 x 3-inch glass loaf pan.

To make the pudding: In a large bowl, combine the flour and ¾ cup of the sugar. In a medium bowl, whisk together the butter, lemon juice, lemon zest, almond extract, egg yolks, and buttermilk. Stir into the dry ingredients until well blended.

Beat the egg whites with an electric mixer until soft peaks form. Gradually beat in the remaining ¼ cup of sugar. Fold the whites into the pudding mixture and transfer the batter to the prepared pan. Place the loaf pan in a large baking pan and add enough hot water to come halfway up the sides of the loaf pan.

Bake for 60 to 70 minutes, or until the top of the pudding is golden and firm to the touch. Remove the loaf pan from the water bath and let cool on a rack for 15 to 20 minutes. Serve warm with one of the fruit sauces.

To make the sauce: In a small saucepan over medium heat, combine 1 cup of the blueberries, ¼ cup of the water, the sugar, and lemon juice. Bring to a boil, stirring frequently, then reduce heat to simmer and cook for 7 to 10 minutes, or until the fruit softens. Stir the cornstarch into the remaining ¼ cup of water until dissolved. Add the cornstarch mixture to the blueberries mixture. Add the remaining 1 cup of blueberries. Cook on low heat for 3 to 4 minutes, or until thickened. Serve immediately, or transfer to a small bowl, cover, and refrigerate for up to 24 hours. **Makes about 2 cups**

Queen of Puddings

Some old-fashioned bread puddings call for bread crumbs instead of buttered slices of bread, such as this pudding dubbed "Queen of Puddings," a dessert my mother made often. After the puddings cooked, she spread the tops of each one with a thin layer of jam and mounded it with meringue. Like most puddings, it can be made in a large buttered baking dish or individually. **Serves 6**

2 cups milk

1 tablespoon unsalted Kerrygold Irish butter

3/4 cup fresh white bread crumbs (see Note)

1/2 cup superfine sugar

Grated zest of 1 lemon

3 large eggs, separated

6 tablespoons strawberry or raspberry preserves, such as Folláin brand (see Resources, page 163)

Preheat the oven to 350°F. Butter six 6-ounce ramekins.

In a large saucepan over medium heat, bring the milk to a boil. Remove from the heat and stir in the butter, bread crumbs, 1/4 cup of the sugar, and the lemon zest. Let sit for 20 minutes, or until the bread crumbs have absorbed the liquid.

In a small bowl, beat the yolks with an electric mixer until light and fluffy. Whisk into the bread crumb mixture. Spoon the mixture into the prepared ramekins. Place the ramekins on a baking sheet and bake for 25 minutes, or until set.

Meanwhile, in a small saucepan over low heat, heat the strawberry preserves for 3 to 5 minutes, or until melted. Remove the puddings from the oven and spoon the preserves over the top. Beat the egg whites with an electric mixer until soft peaks form. Add the remaining 1/4 cup of sugar, one tablespoon at a time, and beat until stiff peaks form. Pile the meringue over the tops of the puddings and swirl into peaks. Return the puddings to the oven. Bake for 10 to 15 minutes, or until the meringues are golden. Serve warm.

NOTE: To make fresh bread crumbs, cut 5 to 6 slices of a stale baguette or rustic bread into 1/2-inch cubes. Put in a blender or a food processor fitted with a grating attachment. Process for 15 to 20 seconds, or until the mixture is ground into fine crumbs. **Makes about 1 cup**

Hazelnut Bavarois

An Irish Bavarian cream, you might ask? Well, yes, if the chef is French and cooking in a Northern Ireland guest house like Beech Hill, County Derry, which prides itself on its eclectic kitchen. This privately owned guest house is set in a charming, leafy suburb of Derry, and has been called one of the best kept secrets of Northern Ireland. Serve the bavarois (pronounced bah-vah-rwah) in stemmed glasses. **Serves 8**

4 large eggs

½ cup sugar

¼ teaspoon salt

One ¼-ounce envelope unflavored gelatin

2½ cups milk

1½ teaspoons vanilla

PRALINE

1 cup sugar

2 tablespoons water

⅔ cup (4 ounces) hazelnuts, chopped

2 cups heavy (whipping) cream

In a large saucepan over medium-low heat, whisk together the eggs, sugar, and salt. Sprinkle the gelatin over the milk to let it soften for a few minutes, then whisk it into the egg mixture. Cook, stirring constantly, for 5 to 7 minutes, or until the mixture is just thick enough to coat the back of a metal spoon (160°F on an instant-read thermometer). Remove from the heat and cool quickly by placing the pan over a bowl filled with ice. Stir in the vanilla. Press a piece of plastic wrap onto the surface of the custard and let stand over the ice for 15 minutes. Remove from the ice and refrigerate for 30 minutes.

To make the praline: Lightly oil a large baking sheet. In a small saucepan over low heat, combine the sugar and water. Cook, stirring constantly, for 4 to 6 minutes, or until the sugar dissolves and gets syrupy. Bring gently to a boil and cook, stirring only once or twice, for 5 to 8 minutes, or until a light amber caramel forms. Stir in the nuts. Quickly pour the mixture into the prepared pan and let cool for 10 to 15 minutes, or until hard. Break the praline into pieces and transfer to a food processor. Process for 15 to 20 seconds, or until the praline is ground into a fine powder.

While the praline is cooling in the pan, whip the cream with an electric mixer until soft peaks form. Fold the whipped cream and praline powder into the custard until blended. Spoon the bavarois into eight 8- or 9-ounce stemmed glasses, cover with plastic wrap, and refrigerate for 1 to 2 hours, or until set.

Garden at Moone High Cross Inn, Moone, County Kildare

Tipsy Pudding in Spiced Wine with Honey Cream Cheese

This light sponge pudding is soaked in spiced wine and poitín, a drink some call "Irish moonshine." The flavor of the pudding might suggest the winter months or even the Christmas season, even though it's seasonless and can be served with a lighter sauce, such as Cabernet Syrup (page 49). Spoon some of the slightly tangy honey cream cheese on top, or for a richer taste, serve it with Crème Fraîche (page 24). **Serves 6**

PUDDING

2 large eggs, separated

¾ cup superfine sugar

2 tablespoons grated lemon rind

1¼ cups fresh white bread crumbs (see Note, page 19)

SPICED WINE

3 cups red wine

Pared zest and juice of 1 lemon

Pared zest and juice of 1 orange

½ cup superfine sugar

1 cinnamon stick

4 whole cloves

1 tablespoon Bunratty Potcheen (see Note)

HONEY CREAM CHEESE

One 3-ounce package cream cheese at room temperature

1 tablespoon honey

1 tablespoon heavy (whipping) cream

To make the pudding: Preheat the oven to 350°F. Butter six 4-ounce ramekins. In a medium bowl, beat the egg yolks, sugar, and lemon rind with an electric mixer for 2 to 3 minutes, or until light and frothy. In a small bowl, beat the egg whites with an electric mixer until stiff peaks form. Stir one quarter of the egg whites into the egg yolk mixture to lighten, then fold in the remaining whites. Fold in the bread crumbs. Spoon the pudding into the prepared ramekins and bake for 20 minutes, or until set. Remove from the oven and cool completely on a wire rack.

To make the spiced wine: In a medium saucepan over medium heat, combine the wine, lemon zest and juice, orange zest and juice, sugar, cinnamon stick, and cloves. Bring to a boil, then reduce the heat to simmer and cook for 8 to 10 minutes, or until reduced slightly. Strain into a clean bowl and stir in the *poitín*.

To make the honey cream cheese: In a small bowl, beat the cream cheese, honey, and cream with an electric mixer until smooth.

To serve, run a knife soaked in hot water around the edge of each dish and unmold the puddings on serving plates or in shallow bowls. Spoon the mulled wine over the puddings until thoroughly soaked. Top with a spoonful of honey cream cheese or Crème Fraîche.

NOTE: The clear liquid known as *poitín* (pronounced potcheen) is a water-clear distillation of barley, sugar, and water sometimes referred to as "Irish Moonshine." Illegal in Ireland since it was banned in 1661, *poitín* was first legalized for export in 1989 by the Bunratty Mead and Liqueur Company of County Clare and branded as Bunratty Potcheen. Permission to sell it in the Irish domestic market was granted in 1997.

Crème Fraîche:

1 cup heavy (whipping) cream

2 tablespoons buttermilk

Combine the cream and buttermilk in a glass container, cover, and let stand at room temperature overnight, or until it becomes very thick. Stir well and refrigerate for up to 10 days. **Makes 1 cup**

Crème Fraîche Whipped Cream:

1 cup heavy (whipping) cream

1 cup Crème Fraîche (above)

1 vanilla bean, split and scraped (see Note, page 14)

2 tablespoons confectioners' sugar

In a medium bowl, combine the cream, crème fraîche, vanilla bean scrapings, and confectioners' sugar. Beat with an electric mixer until soft peaks form. **Makes about 2 cups**

IRISH HONEY

Honey experts claim it has been in existence since as early as 7000 B.C., when cave paintings were created in Spain depicting beekeeping. Ancient Egyptians used honey as a sweetener, Greek recipe books contained sweetmeats and cakes made from honey, and Romans used it as a gift to the gods. Honey continued to be of importance in Europe until the Renaissance, when sugar arrived and was discovered to be a suitable substitute.

While sugar began to replace honey in many recipes, Irish cookery writer Theodora FitzGibbon revered honey for its "lovely wild taste . . . the sweetness of a sort which can never be obtained with sugar." Today, honey is again popular and has become the natural choice for bakers who appreciate its distinct flavor. Honey adds a golden hue to crust and crumb alike, and because it attracts and absorbs moisture, honey keeps baked goods moist and helps them stay fresh longer. There are several forms of honey available in Ireland—liquid, whipped, comb, and cut comb—derived from a wide range of floral sources.

One brand, Mileeven, has grown steadily since 1986, when a beekeeping hobby turned into a specialty food company. Mileeven supplies a niche market with "specialist" honeys, including those flavored with Irish Mist liqueur and Jameson Irish whiskey, and a range of other products such as fruits preserved in honey, jams, and marmalades. Folláin, Mologa, Boyne Valley, Natural Ireland, and Lios Na Graí are other Irish honeys to look for. (See Resources, page 163.)

Celtic Rice Pudding with Raisin Sauce

Old-fashioned rice pudding, which seems to transcend international boundaries, is made distinctively Irish with the addition of Celtic Crossing Liqueur, a blend of Irish malt whiskeys and French cognac. First launched in 1996, it was produced to commemorate the 150th anniversary of the Irish famine and to honor those who had to leave Ireland to seek new lives elsewhere. The popular liqueur also makes a major contribution to desserts like this traditional rice pudding served with raisin sauce. **Serves 8**

PUDDING

4 cups milk

1 teaspoon vanilla

²/₃ cup heavy (whipping) cream

²/₃ cup Arborio rice

¹/₃ cup sugar

¹/₄ cup Celtic Crossing Liqueur

2 large eggs, beaten

1 teaspoon ground cinnamon

RAISIN SAUCE

³/₄ cup Celtic Crossing Liqueur

¹/₂ cup golden raisins

¹/₂ cup sugar

2 tablespoons water

4 tablespoons unsalted Kerrygold Irish butter, cut into small pieces

¹/₄ cup heavy (whipping) cream

To make the pudding: In a large saucepan over medium heat, combine the milk, vanilla, and cream. Bring to a boil, then stir in the rice and sugar. Reduce the heat to low and simmer, stirring frequently, for 30 minutes, or until the rice is tender.

Preheat the oven to 350°F. Butter a 9-inch square glass baking dish.

In a small bowl, whisk together the Celtic Crossing, eggs, and cinnamon. Stir into the rice mixture. Pour the combined mixture into the prepared pan and bake for 60 to 75 minutes, or until the pudding is set and the top is golden. Remove from the oven and let cool on a wire rack while making the sauce.

To make the raisin sauce: In a small saucepan over medium heat, combine the Celtic Crossing and raisins. Cook for 5 minutes, or until the raisins are tender. Cover and let stand for 10 minutes.

In another small saucepan over low heat, combine the sugar and water. Cook, stirring constantly, for 2 to 3 minutes, or until the sugar dissolves. Increase the heat to high and boil, without stirring, for 4 to 6 minutes, or until a light amber caramel forms. Remove from the heat and whisk in the butter and cream. Stir in the raisin mixture and cook over low heat for 2 to 4 minutes, or until thickened. To serve, spoon the pudding into bowls or stemmed glasses and spoon the sauce on top.

Steel-Cut Oat Pudding

Oatmeal is more than simply a favorite breakfast cereal, especially in Ireland, where it's becoming increasingly popular as a recipe ingredient. McCann's brand, made in Sallins, County Kildare, produces several types of oatmeal, including instant and quick-cooking (to find out the difference, see page 77), but their steel-cut oats, which are whole-grain groats, are perhaps their most exceptional. Golden in color, these pinhead oats resemble mini rice particles. Their distinctive crunchy texture makes them perfect for puddings and other sweets. **Serves 6 to 8**

---

1 cup McCann's steel-cut oatmeal, toasted (see Note)

4 cups water

1 cup milk

2 large eggs

¾ cup light brown sugar

2 tablespoons unsalted Kerrygold Irish butter, melted

1 tablespoon grated orange zest

¼ teaspoon ground nutmeg

½ cup golden raisins, chopped

2 tablespoons Baileys Irish Cream

Crème Fraîche (optional, page 24), for serving

Preheat the oven to 350°F. Butter a 1½-quart casserole or soufflé dish.

In a medium saucepan over high heat, combine the oats and water. Bring to a boil, then reduce the heat to a simmer and cook, stirring frequently, for 20 minutes, or until the liquid is absorbed.

In a large bowl, whisk together the milk, eggs, sugar, butter, orange zest, and nutmeg. Stir in the raisins and Baileys, then stir in the oat mixture. Pour into the prepared dish and bake for 35 to 40 minutes, or until lightly browned and set. Serve warm with Crème Fraîche, if desired.

NOTE: To toast steel-cut oats, preheat the oven to 300°F. Spread out the oats in a pie plate, and bake for approximately 20 minutes. Unused toasted oats can be stored in a tightly covered container for future use.

Chocolate Truffle Cakes with Raspberry Sauce

Chocoholics will not be disappointed by these molten chocolate cakes with pudding-like centers surrounded by decadent sponge exteriors. It's restaurant dessert at its finest—you'll find some variation of it in most Irish restaurants, including La Stampa, in Dublin, Castle Leslie, in County Monaghan, and from Ballynahinch Castle, in County Galway, where this recipe is from. But they are uncomplicated enough for any home cook to prepare for a special occasion. Make the batter about 12 hours before you plan to bake it. Serve the cakes with the raspberry sauce or with Lemon Curd Cream (page 107) if you like the sweet-tart combination of chocolate and lemon. **Serves 6**

CAKES

6 ounces bittersweet (not unsweetened) or semisweet chocolate

¾ cup (1½ sticks) unsalted Kerrygold Irish butter

1 cup superfine sugar

1 tablespoon cornstarch

4 large eggs

4 large egg yolks

1 teaspoon orange extract

RASPBERRY SAUCE

2 cups fresh raspberries

6 tablespoons sugar

1½ tablespoons cornstarch

1½ tablespoons water

To make the cakes: In a medium saucepan over medium-low heat, combine the chocolate and butter. Melt, stirring constantly, for 5 minutes, or until smooth. In a small bowl, combine the superfine sugar and cornstarch. Stir into the chocolate mixture. Remove from the heat and let cool. In a medium bowl, beat the eggs and egg yolks with an electric mixer for 4 to 5 minutes, or until pale and thickened. Stir in the orange extract. Combine the chocolate mixture with the egg mixture, transfer to a large bowl, cover, and refrigerate for 10 to 12 hours to let the batter thicken.

To make the raspberry sauce: Put the raspberries in a food processor or blender and process for 10 to 20 seconds, or until puréed. Pass through a fine mesh sieve to remove the seeds. Transfer to a small saucepan and cook over medium-low heat for 2 minutes, or until heated through. Stir in the sugar and cook for 5 minutes, or until the sugar dissolves completely. In a small bowl, whisk together the cornstarch and water. Stir into the raspberry mixture and cook for 2 to 3 minutes, or until slightly thickened. Let cool, then refrigerate for up to 2 days.

Preheat the oven to 300°F. Butter six 6-ounce ramekins and dust with flour. Tap out the excess.

Spoon the batter into the prepared ramekins and bake for 15 minutes, or until the tops are crusty (the centers will still be runny). Remove from the oven and let cool on a wire rack for 5 minutes.

To serve, run a knife around the inside of each ramekin. Lift out the cake and transfer to a dessert plate. Put a spoonful of sauce on each plate.

Buttermilk Pudding with Strawberry-Rhubarb Compote

Once upon a time, a pudding like this might have been made from carrageen, a seaweed that some call "a gift to Irish kitchens from the sea." Dark green or purple in color, it's pulled off rocks along the coastlines of Ireland, then dried and bleached. Also known as "Irish moss" or "sea moss," carrageen has a gelatinous quality that makes it perfect for thickening puddings, jellies, and soups. A bit like old-fashioned carrageen pudding, this recipe uses buttermilk for flavor and gelatin for firming. Serve the pudding, reminiscent of blancmange or Italian panna cotta, with the sweet-tart strawberry-rhubarb compote. **Serves 4**

PUDDING

2 cups buttermilk

One ¼-ounce envelope unflavored gelatin

⅔ cup heavy (whipping) cream

¼ cup sugar

1 tablespoon grated lemon zest

STRAWBERRY-RHUBARB COMPOTE

1½ cups sugar

1¼ cups water

1 pound rhubarb, cut into 1-inch pieces

2 cups sliced fresh strawberries

6 tablespoons confectioners' sugar

To make the pudding: Spray four 6-ounce ramekins with cooking oil spray. In the top of a double boiler over simmering water, combine the buttermilk and gelatin. Stir until the gelatin dissolves. Set aside.

In a small saucepan over medium heat, combine the cream, sugar, and lemon zest. Bring to a boil, then reduce the heat to low and simmer for 1 to 2 minutes, or until slightly thickened. Remove from the heat, then stir into the buttermilk mixture. Strain through a fine mesh sieve into a clean bowl, then cool quickly by placing the bowl over a larger bowl filled with ice. When cool, pour into the prepared dishes and refrigerate for at least 6 hours, or until the puddings are set.

To make the compote: In a small saucepan over medium heat, combine the sugar and water. Bring to a boil and cook for 2 minutes. Reduce heat to low, add the rhubarb and strawberries, and cook for 10 minutes, or until the fruit is tender. Remove from the heat and let cool completely. Transfer to a bowl, cover, and refrigerate for at least 1 hour and up to 24 hours.

To serve, run a knife that has been dipped into hot water around the insides of the ramekins and unmold onto dessert plates. Spoon the compote around the puddings.

THE HIDDEN IRELAND

Ballymaloe House, Shanagarry,
County Cork

The Hidden Ireland is a unique collection of beautiful and historic private houses located throughout Ireland. They are—emphatically—not hotels or guest houses, but private homes of great character and history. Many of the hosts and hostesses have special interests like wine, antiques, riding, or fishing, which they look forward to sharing with guests. Some of the houses are at the center of great Irish estates—Bantry House, Ballinkeeke, and Temple House, to name but a few—while others were designed by famous architects and built for or lived in by famous figures from Ireland's past: Delphi Lodge was originally the sporting playground of the Marquis of Sligo, and No. 31, located in the heart of Georgian Dublin at 31 Leeson Close, is the former home of Ireland's leading architect Sam Stephenson.

Some houses are small—four to five rooms, perhaps, like Glenlohane, Emlaghmore Lodge, Ballyvolane, or Glenview House—but surrounded by manicured gardens, lawns for croquet, tennis courts, or swimming pools. Many of the houses have belonged to the same families for generations. Regardless of the location or size of the properties, the Hidden Ireland provides a unique and fascinating alternative to conventional tourist accommodations and crowded restaurants. These residences provide good food and wine, which are enhanced by the charm of the surroundings. (See Resources, page 163.)

Sticky Toffee Sponge Pudding

More a cake than a pudding, Merrie Greene's version of the famous Anglo-Irish dessert known as Sticky Toffee Pudding is (sort of) steamed like its original counterparts, but with a covering of foil rather than in a traditional mold or pudding tin. As hostess at Ballyvolane House, an Italianate-style country mansion in Castleyons, County Cork, Mrs. Greene does all the cooking while husband Jeremy looks after the guests. Ballyvolane is a member of the charming group of Irish country homes called the Hidden Ireland (see page 29). Situated close to the Cork Blackwater, Ireland's premier salmon river, it's a favorite retreat for anglers. **Serves 6 to 8**

PUDDING

1½ cups (6 ounces) chopped dates

1 cup water

1 teaspoon baking soda

4 tablespoons unsalted Kerrygold Irish butter

¾ cup sugar

2 large eggs

½ teaspoon vanilla extract

1½ cups self-rising flour

TOFFEE SAUCE

2 cups heavy (whipping) cream

½ cup packed dark brown sugar

2 tablespoons molasses or dark corn syrup

To make the pudding: Preheat the oven to 350°F. Butter a 4- to 5-cup soufflé dish or decorative pudding mold. In a saucepan over medium heat, combine the dates and water. Bring to a boil, then stir in the baking soda. (The mixture will foam up.) Remove from the heat and let cool.

In a large bowl, cream the butter and sugar with an electric mixer until pale and fluffy. Beat in the eggs and vanilla. Fold in the flour and date mixture. Pour into the prepared dish or mold, cover loosely with foil, and bake for 40 to 45 minutes, or until firm. Remove from the oven, transfer to a wire rack, and let cool for 10 minutes.

While the pudding is baking, make the toffee sauce: In a medium saucepan over medium heat, combine the cream, brown sugar, and molasses. Cook for 8 to 10 minutes, or until the sauce is thickened.

To serve, invert the dish or mold onto a plate and pour some of the sauce over the top. Cut the pudding into slices and serve with the remaining sauce.

Irish Mist Soufflés

The essential ingredients in an old-fashioned pudding—eggs, milk, sugar, flavorings—are basically the same as those in a soufflé, except, of course, in a soufflé the eggs are separated, the whites whipped, and flour or cream of tartar is added to hold it together and puff it up to an ethereal delight. Liqueurs are often used for flavoring dessert soufflés, so it comes as no surprise that Irish Mist—a blend of spirits, Irish honey, and exotic herbs—has become the flavor of choice to offer a native touch to the classic French dish. **Serves 8**

3 tablespoons unsalted Kerrygold Irish butter

9 tablespoons sugar

¼ cup all-purpose flour

Pinch of salt

1¼ cups milk

3 large egg yolks, lightly beaten

¼ cup Irish Mist liqueur

1 teaspoon vanilla extract

5 large egg whites

Preheat the oven to 375°F. Butter eight 6-ounce ramekins and dust with 3 tablespoons (about 1 generous teaspoon each) of the sugar. Tap out the excess.

In a large saucepan over medium heat, melt the butter. Whisk in the flour, 1 teaspoon at a time, and the salt until well blended. Slowly whisk in the milk. Cook, stirring constantly, for 1 to 2 minutes, or until thickened.

Remove from the heat and stir in 4 tablespoons of the sugar. Whisk in the egg yolks, Irish Mist, and vanilla. Set aside and let cool.

Combine the egg whites and remaining 2 tablespoons of the sugar in a medium clean, dry bowl. Beat with an electric mixer until soft peaks form. Fold one quarter of the whites into the yolk mixture to lighten it. Fold in the remaining whites until blended. Spoon the soufflé mixture into the prepared ramekins and place in a baking pan. Add enough hot water to come halfway up the side of the dishes. Bake for 30 minutes, or until the tops are browned and the soufflés are risen and set. Serve immediately.

IRISH MIST AND TULLAMORE DEW

The B. Daly whiskey distillery was established in Tullamore, County Offaly, in 1829. When Daniel E. Williams eventually took over the company in 1897, he created its signature brand, Tullamore Dew, a whiskey to which he gave his initials.

In 1947, Daniel's grandson Desmond launched Ireland's first liqueur, Irish Mist, a combination of Tullamore Dew Irish whiskey, honey, and herbs. The recipe for Irish Mist, inspired by the drink of the ancient Irish chieftains called heather wine, disappeared for centuries with the great exodus of the Irish earls, an event that has passed into Irish history as "the Flight of the Wild Geese." Apparently, European travelers visiting Ireland offered an old manuscript to Williams, who recognized it as the ancient recipe for heather wine. Today, the Tullamore Dew Heritage Center, housed in the original warehouse of the old distillery, celebrates the people and the place that created one of the world's great Irish whiskeys and Ireland's original liqueur. Located at Bury Quay in the heart of Tullamore, the center also chronicles the story of the development of Tullamore and its place in the Irish midlands. It's open daily year-round for tours and tasting. (See Resources, page 163.)

Locke's Distillery, Kilbeggan,
County Westmeath

IRISH COFFEE

In 1943, chef-barman Joe Sheridan decided that a blend of cream, hot coffee, and Irish whiskey would make a perfect welcoming drink for cold and weary passengers arriving at the town of Foynes, in County Limerick, from the United States on the "flying boats," the first transatlantic passenger planes. He wanted the drink to be warm and welcoming, Irish in character, and sophisticated enough to appeal to international travelers. After many experiments over a number of years, including the addition of sugar, Joe Sheridan finally came up with the recipe for what would become the quintessential Irish drink. When Shannon International Airport opened in 1947, Irish coffee became its official beverage.

In the early 1950s, *San Francisco Chronicle* journalist Stan Delaplane enjoyed an Irish coffee at Shannon and introduced it to America at his favorite watering hole, the Buena Vista Café near Fisherman's Wharf. Irish coffee soon became the drink of San Francisco. Since its introduction in 1952, more than fifteen million have been served at that popular restaurant alone, and millions more elsewhere.

Joe Sheridan's original recipe, which is still used at the Buena Vista, is as follows: Heat a stemmed heat-proof goblet by running it under very hot water. Pour in 1 jigger of Irish whiskey. Add 3 cubes of sugar and fill the goblet with strong black coffee to within 1 inch of the brim. Stir to dissolve the sugar. Top off with lightly whipped cream. Do not stir after adding the cream, as the true flavor is obtained by drinking the hot mixture through the cream. *Sláinte!*

Traditional painted caravan,
Dingle Penninsula, County Kerry

Irish Coffee Crèmes Caramels with Irish Coffee Sauce

A classic dessert, crème caramel—also known as crème renversée in France, crema caramella in Italy, and flan in Spain—is a custard that's baked in a caramel-coated ramekin or mold. When the chilled custard is turned out onto a dessert plate, the custard is glazed and sauced with the caramel. Although not necessarily new to Irish baking, this recipe, from chef Marie Harding of Lovett's Restaurant, in Douglas, County Cork, is an all-Irish interpretation that includes Irish whiskey in a coffee-flavored base. Serves 6

CRÈMES CARAMELS

½ cup plus 1 tablespoon sugar

½ cup strong black coffee

1 tablespoon Irish whiskey

2 cups milk

1 tablespoon instant coffee powder

2 large eggs

2 large egg yolks

2 tablespoons Irish whiskey

IRISH COFFEE SAUCE

2 teaspoons instant coffee

⅔ cup boiling water

1 cup sugar

¼ to ⅔ cup cold water

1 tablespoon Irish whiskey

To make the crèmes caramels: In a small saucepan over medium-high heat, combine ½ cup of the sugar and the coffee. Cook for 3 to 5 minutes, stirring constantly, or until the sugar begins to caramelize and thicken. Add the whiskey and stir until smooth. Divide the coffee mixture among six 4-ounce ramekins and freeze for 1 to 2 hours, or until the caramel is firm.

Preheat the oven to 325°F. In a medium saucepan over medium-high heat, combine the milk and instant coffee. Bring to a boil, stirring constantly. Whisk together the eggs, yolks, remaining tablespoon of sugar, and the whiskey in a medium bowl and slowly stir it into the hot milk. Cook for 5 minutes, or until the mixture thickens. Spoon the custard into the ramekins and place in a baking pan. Add enough boiling water to come halfway up the side of the dishes. Bake for 45 to 50 minutes, or until the custard is browned and nearly set. Remove the dishes from the pan and cool completely on a wire rack. Cover and then refrigerate until cold, for at least 3 hours and up to 24 hours.

To make the Irish coffee sauce: In a small bowl, combine the instant coffee and boiling water and stir until dissolved. Set aside. In a small saucepan over medium heat, combine the sugar and cold water. Bring to a low boil, and cook for 2 to 3 minutes, or until syrupy. Add the coffee mixture and cook, stirring constantly, for 5 minutes, or until the caramel has dissolved. Add the whiskey, cool completely, transfer to a bowl, then refrigerate.

To serve, dip the bottoms of the ramekins into hot water to loosen the caramel. Run a knife around the inside of the dishes and invert the custards onto dessert plates. Drizzle some of the sauce around each custard.

Blueberry Crèmes Brûlées

The ever-versatile blueberry shines in these crèmes brûlées from Noel McMeel, head chef at Castle Leslie, Glaslough, in County Monaghan, the venue for Paul McCartney's 2002 wedding. If you like, add a crumble topping of digestive biscuits, such as Carr's or McVities' brand, in place of the caramelized sugar. **Serves 6**

1 cup fresh blueberries

2 cups half-and-half

Grated zest and juice of 1 lemon

5 large egg yolks

½ cup plus 1 tablespoon sugar

Pinch of ground nutmeg

Preheat the oven to 325°F. Divide the blueberries among six 4-ounce ramekins.

In a large saucepan over medium heat, bring the half-and-half to a gentle boil. Stir in the grated lemon zest. In a large bowl, whisk together the egg yolks, ½ cup of the sugar, the lemon juice, and nutmeg. Stir one quarter of the half-and-half into the egg mixture, then stir the egg mixture into the half-and-half. Spoon the custard into the prepared ramekins and place in a baking pan. Add enough boiling water to come halfway up the side of the dishes. Bake for 55 to 60 minutes, or until the custard is set. Remove the dishes from the pan and cool completely on a wire rack. Cover and refrigerate until cold, for at least 3 hours and up to 48 hours.

Preheat the broiler. Sprinkle each custard with some of the remaining 1 tablespoon of sugar. Place under the broiler 4 inches from the heat source for 1 to 2 minutes, or use a kitchen blowtorch and move the flame constantly over the surface until the sugar melts, bubbles, and lightly browns.

Apple farm, Moorestown, County Tipperary

The Olde Bakery, Killarney,
County Kerry

CHAPTER TWO

tarts

Ireland's Brehon laws, or laws of the Fianna, were formulated about A.D. 438 and served as ancient rules of hospitality. According to the Brehon law, people in higher stations were bound to entertain guests without asking any questions, and the master of the house was obliged to keep his kitchen fire constantly burning in readiness for the arrival of strangers. Among the choices that might be offered to a stranger: a good piece of beef, eggs and milk, sugar and nutmeg, fresh butter, a good loaf, and a finely made tart.

Pastry making apparently came to Ireland with the Normans, so many of the same fruits used in pudding making were used for pies and tarts as well. When I finally started to bake pastries, I only made tarts. The reason: only one crust to deal with! I particularly liked galettes, a free-form, willy-nilly kind of tart that was so forgiving stylistically I felt I was infallible. I also liked making tarts because they were seasonless, open to any number of interpretations, and easy to embellish with a big scoop of ice cream, some freshly whipped sweet cream, or with crème fraîche, one of the most luxurious of all tart toppings.

Irish chefs love them, too. In many cases, a tart will be presented at a restaurant as a single-serving tartlet with some thick custard or fruit coulis drizzled around the plate to pretty it up. For the purposes of this cookbook, however, most of the recipes are for full-size desserts baked in 9- or 10-inch loose-bottomed tart pans, quiche pans, or springform pans. Many of the recipes can be made as tartlets though, so feel free to experiment. In most cases, a recipe for one tart crust will make 4 to 6 four-inch tartlet crusts and as many as 20 bite-size pastries baked in 2¾-inch pans. Reduce the baking time by 10 to 15 minutes for tartlets.

Soda Bread Tarte Tatin with Cashel Blue and Cider Ice

The original tarte Tatin is a French upside-down apple tart cooked in a skillet or baking dish. The bottom of the pan is covered with butter and sugar, which caramelizes on the stove top, then topped with apples and a pastry crust. After baking, the tart is inverted onto a serving plate, and the caramel then becomes the topping. The tart was invented over one hundred years ago by the Tatin sisters, Fanny and Caroline, in Lamotte-Beuvron, France, while cooking at their family's hotel. The girls apparently forgot to put the crust in the tart pan, so they put it on top of the fruit, then flipped it over. The technique has been adapted by many cooks, using a variety of fruits. Derry Clarke, chef-proprietor of L'Ecrivain, in Dublin, gives it a distinctly Irish identity by topping his version with a soda bread crust and serving it with Cashel Blue and cider ice, a lemony sorbet spiked with Tipperary-made blue cheese and cider. Make the ice at least 6 hours before you plan to serve it. Alternatively, top the tart with vanilla ice cream, if you wish. **Serves 8 to 10**

CASHEL BLUE AND CIDER ICE

1 pint frozen lemon sorbet, softened slightly

¾ cup Magners Irish cider, or similar fermented cider

3 ounces Cashel Blue or similar blue cheese, crumbled

6 tablespoons heavy (whipping) cream

SODA BREAD CRUST

¼ cup golden raisins

¼ cup Irish whiskey

2 cups cake flour

1 tablespoon baking powder

¼ cup sugar

½ cup (1 stick) unsalted Kerrygold Irish butter

½ cup buttermilk

FILLING

1 cup superfine sugar

4 tablespoons unsalted Kerrygold Irish butter

1 tablespoon ground cardamom

2 Granny Smith apples, peeled, cored, and sliced crosswise (about 16 slices)

To make the ice: Spoon softened sorbet into a blender or food processor. Add the cider, blue cheese, and cream. Process until smooth, then transfer to a plastic container, cover, and freeze for 6 hours, or until firm.

To make the crust: In a small bowl, combine the raisins and whiskey and soak for 30 minutes. In a large bowl, sift together the cake flour, baking powder, and sugar. With a pastry cutter, 2 knives, or your fingers, work or cut in the butter until it resembles coarse crumbs. Drain the raisins and reserve the whiskey for the filling. Stir in the raisins and buttermilk and mix well until the dough comes together.

Dust a work surface with flour. Turn out the dough, and with floured hands, form it into a ball. Knead for 20 seconds, then roll or pat the dough into a circle 12 inches in diameter. Preheat the oven to 400°F.

(continued)

Soda Bread Tarte Tatin with Cashel Blue and Cider Ice *(continued)*

To make the filling: In a 10-inch ovenproof, nonstick skillet, combine the superfine sugar, reserved whiskey from the crust, the butter, and cardamom. Cook over medium-low heat for 2 to 3 minutes, or until the butter melts and the sugar caramelizes. Add the apple slices and cook, in batches, for 2 to 3 minutes, or until tender. Remove the apples with a slotted spoon and continue to cook the butter and sugar for 3 to 5 minutes, or until the caramel thickens. Starting in the center, arrange the apple slices in concentric circles over the caramel.

Place the dough on top of the apples, tucking it around at the edge of the pan. Bake the tart for about 15 minutes, or until the crust is golden. Remove from the oven and let cool on a wire rack for 10 minutes. Place a rimmed serving plate over the pan. With potholders to protect your hands, invert the tart onto the plate and remove the pan. Slice the tart and serve warm with Cashel Blue and cider ice.

Cottage with garden art, near Newgrange, County Meath

Apple Tart with Hazelnut Crust and Crumble

In this tart apples are combined with hazelnuts, also one of the oldest ingredients in Irish cooking, which go into the crust as well as the crumble topping. The crust, a no-roll pastry similar to cookie dough, is a snap to make and is pressed into the pan with your fingertips; the crumble is similar to those you'll find in Chapter Three. Serve the tart with Crème Fraîche Whipped Cream (page 24), if you wish. **Serves 8 to 10**

CRUST

1 cup chopped hazelnuts

½ cup (1 stick) unsalted Kerrygold Irish butter at room temperature

2½ tablespoons sugar

1½ cups all-purpose flour

1 large egg, beaten

½ teaspoon vanilla extract

FILLING

4 to 5 large apples (a combination of tart and sweet)

1 cup sugar

2 tablespoons cornstarch

2 teaspoons ground cinnamon

3 tablespoons unsalted Kerrygold Irish butter

TOPPING

½ cup light brown sugar

⅔ cup all-purpose flour

1 teaspoon ground cinnamon

½ cup (1 stick) cold unsalted Kerrygold Irish butter, cut into small pieces

½ cup chopped hazelnuts

Crème Fraîche Whipped Cream (optional, page 24) for serving

To make the crust: Butter a 10-inch deep-dish pie pan. Combine the hazelnuts, butter, sugar, and flour in a food processor fitted with a metal blade. Pulse 8 to 12 times, or until the mixture resembles coarse crumbs. Add the egg and vanilla and process for 15 to 20 seconds, or until the dough comes together. Gather into a ball, and with floured hands, press it onto the bottom and up the sides of the prepared pan. Refrigerate for 30 minutes.

Preheat the oven to 350°F. Cover the crust with a pie crust shield (see Note). Bake for 20 to 25 minutes, or until golden brown. Remove from the oven and let cool on a wire rack. Maintain the oven temperature.

To make the filling: Peel, core, and slice the apples. In a large bowl, combine the apples, sugar, cornstarch, and cinnamon. Toss to coat the fruit. Spoon the fruit into the crust and dot with butter. Bake for 20 to 25 minutes, or until the fruit is tender.

Meanwhile, make the topping: In a small bowl, combine the brown sugar, flour, cinnamon, and butter. Blend with a fork until the mixture resembles coarse crumbs. Stir in the hazelnuts. Sprinkle the mixture over the fruit. Remove the pie crust shield. Bake the pie for 20 minutes more, or until the topping is golden. Remove from the oven and let cool on a wire rack for about 10 minutes.

NOTE: A pie crust shield is a ring of heavy-duty, non-stick coated metal that sits on top of a tart or pie. It keeps the edges of the crust from burning before the middle is done. It is especially helpful when prebaking pie crust shells for tarts, and can also be used when baking quiches and double-crust pies.

Rhubarb Tarte Tatin

Carlingford, in County Louth, is often called "Kinsale of the northeast," referring to its reputation for fine food like its County Cork counterpart. Ghan House, a stunning Georgian guest house in the heart of the medieval town, makes a big contribution to such acclaim. Under the direction of the Carroll family, the hotel dining room features the best of local ingredients, hosts "gourmet nights," and even operates a cookery school where guest chefs provide cookery demonstrations. This tart, however, is from resident chef Chris Diggins, and it is a favorite in spring, when rhubarb is at its peak. **Serves 8 to 10**

CRUST

1¼ cups all-purpose flour

½ cup (1 stick) cold unsalted Kerrygold Irish butter, cut into small pieces

2 tablespoons sugar

1 large egg

1 to 2 tablespoons ice water

FILLING

6 tablespoons unsalted Kerrygold Irish butter

½ cup sugar

1 pound rhubarb, trimmed and sliced

Crème Fraîche (optional, page 24) for topping

To start the crust: Combine the flour, butter, and sugar in a food processor fitted with a metal blade. Pulse 8 to 10 times, or until the mixture resembles coarse crumbs. Add the egg and water and process for 15 to 20 seconds, or until the dough comes together. Turn out the dough onto a floured work surface, form it into a ball, then wrap in plastic wrap and refrigerate for 1 hour.

To make the filling: Preheat the oven to 425°F. Butter a 10-inch quiche pan. In a large skillet over medium heat, melt the butter. Stir in the sugar and cook, stirring constantly, for 4 to 6 minutes, or until the sugar dissolves. Add the rhubarb, reduce the heat to medium-low, and cook, stirring occasionally, for 10 to 12 minutes, or until the rhubarb is tender. Transfer to the prepared pan.

Dust a work surface with flour. Roll out the dough to a circle 12 inches in diameter. Place the pastry over the fruit, tucking it around the fruit at the edge of the pan. Bake for 20 to 23 minutes, or until golden. Remove from the oven and transfer to a wire rack. Let the tart cool for 10 minutes. Place a rimmed serving plate over the pan. With potholders to protect your hands, invert the tart onto the plate and remove the pan. Slice the tart and serve warm with Crème Fraîche, if desired.

Ghan Cottage, Carlingford, County Louth

Delphi Plum Tart with Hazelnut Praline and Cabernet Syrup

Jeff McCourt, chef at the Mountain Resort and Spa at Delphi in Leenane, County Galway, uses a simple puff pastry crust for his plum tart, then embellishes it by serving it with crumbled hazelnut praline and cabernet syrup. Prepare the praline and syrup before assembling the tart. **Serves 6 to 8**

CABERNET SYRUP

1 cup sugar

1 cup cabernet wine

HAZELNUT PRALINE

1 cup sugar

2 tablespoons water

⅔ cup (4 ounces) hazelnuts, chopped

TART

2 tablespoons unsalted Kerrygold Irish butter

½ cup packed light brown sugar

1 vanilla bean, split and scraped (see Note, page 14)

6 to 8 red plums, halved and pitted

1 sheet frozen puff pastry from a 17.3-ounce package, left at room temperature for 30 minutes (see Note)

To make the syrup: In a small saucepan over medium heat, combine the sugar and wine. Bring to a boil, then reduce the heat to low and cook for 10 to 12 minutes, or until reduced by half and syrupy. Set aside to cool.

To make the praline: Line a baking sheet with waxed paper. In a small saucepan over low heat, combine the sugar and water. Cook, stirring constantly, for 4 to 6 minutes, or until the sugar dissolves and is syrupy. Bring gently to a boil, and cook, stirring once or twice, for 5 to 8 minutes, or until a light amber caramel forms. Stir in the hazelnuts. Quickly pour the mixture onto the prepared plate and let cool for 10 to 15 minutes, or until hardened. When hardened, place a second sheet of waxed paper on top of the praline and crush it into small pieces with a rolling pin.

To make the tart: Preheat the oven to 400°F. In a 10-inch ovenproof, nonstick skillet, melt the butter over medium heat. Stir in the brown sugar and vanilla bean scrapings and cook for 5 to 8 minutes, or until the mixture

caramelizes slightly. Starting in the center of the pan, arrange the plums, cut side down, in concentric circles.

Dust a work surface with flour. Roll out 1 sheet of puff pastry to a circle 12 inches in diameter. Place the pastry over the plum mixture, tucking it around the plums at the edge of the pan.

Bake the tart for 25 minutes, or until the pastry is puffed and golden. Remove the tart from the oven and let cool for 10 minutes on a wire rack. Place a rimmed serving plate over the pan. With potholders to protect your hands, invert the tart onto the plate and remove the pan.

Slice the tart. Drizzle a little of the syrup around each slice and sprinkle with the praline.

NOTE: Reserve the remaining sheet of puff pastry for another use by wrapping it well in plastic and storing in the freezer.

Pear Tart with Almond Cream

There's something luxurious about a dessert that includes a rich almond cream, also known as frangipane or frangipani. When the cream is used in tarts pears, apples, and apricots are perfect mates. (See the variations that follow.) **Serves 8 to 10**

CRUST

1¾ cups all-purpose flour

½ cup (1 stick) cold Kerrygold Irish butter, cut into small pieces

1 tablespoon sugar

Pinch of salt

3 to 5 tablespoons ice water

FILLING

½ cup (1 stick) unsalted Kerrygold Irish butter at room temperature

½ cup sugar

2 large eggs

½ cup finely ground almonds

2 teaspoons all-purpose flour

1 teaspoon vanilla extract

½ teaspoon almond extract

3 firm, ripe Bartlett or Anjou pears, peeled, cored, halved, and cut into ¼-inch slices

⅓ cup apricot preserves

1 teaspoon water

To start the crust: Combine the flour, butter, sugar, and salt in a food processor fitted with a metal blade. Pulse 8 to 10 times, or until the mixture resembles coarse crumbs. Add 3 tablespoons of the water and pulse just until the dough comes together. Add remaining water if necessary. Dust a work surface with flour. Turn out the dough, form it into a ball, then wrap in plastic wrap and refrigerate for 1 hour. Remove the dough from the refrigerator 10 minutes before rolling.

To make the filling: Cream the butter and sugar together with an electric mixer. Beat in the eggs, one at a time, then the almonds, flour, vanilla extract, and almond extract.

Preheat the oven to 350°F. Butter a 10-inch tart pan with a removable bottom. Roll out the dough to a circle 12 inches in diameter. Transfer to the prepared pan, fold excess dough in, and press with your fingers to form thick sides.

Pour the filling into the crust. Starting in the center, arrange the pear slices in concentric circles over the filling. Bake the tart for 35 to 40 minutes, or until the filling is puffed and browned and the pears are tender. Remove from the oven and transfer to a wire rack.

In a small saucepan over medium heat, combine the apricot preserves and water. Heat for 3 to 5 minutes, or until bubbling. Brush the apricot mixture over the top of the pears while the tart is still hot. Cool the tart in the pan before releasing the side.

Variations

Apple Tart with Almond Cream: For the pears, substitute 2 large Granny Smith apples, peeled, cored, and sliced, and proceed with the recipe.

Apricot and Almond Tart: Dublin chef Patrick McLarnon makes a frangipane tart with dried apricots. Substitute about 18 apricots for the pears. Split them in half lengthwise and soak them in hot water for about 20 minutes. Drain and squeeze out any excess water. Proceed with the recipe, but scatter the apricots directly over the crust, spoon the filling over the top, and bake.

Strawberry-Rhubarb Galette

Strawberry-rhubarb pie is a staple of Nick's Warehouse, in Belfast, County Antrim, from the moment the season's first crop of rhubarb is picked in April. Chef-proprietor Nick Price's recipe is perfect for a rustic tart or galette, and it's easy to assemble when frozen puff pastry substitutes for the traditional pastry crust. **Serves 8 to 10**

1 sheet frozen puff pastry from a 17.3-ounce package, left at room temperature for 30 minutes (see Note)

5 to 6 stalks rhubarb, cut into ¼-inch pieces

¾ cup fresh strawberries, hulled and sliced

½ cup sugar

3 tablespoons cornstarch

1 tablespoon unsalted Kerrygold Irish butter, melted

Confectioners' sugar for dusting

Crème Fraîche Whipped Cream (optional, page 24) for topping

Preheat the oven to 400°F. Butter a 9- or 10-inch tart pan with a removable bottom and place on a baking sheet. Dust a work surface with flour. Roll out the pastry to a circle 12 inches in diameter. Transfer to the prepared pan, pressing the dough onto the bottom and up the sides of the pan, leaving a 2-inch overhang.

In a large bowl, combine the rhubarb, strawberries, sugar, and cornstarch. Spoon the filling into the pan. Fold the overhanging pastry border over the fruit and press it into a scalloped or pleated border. Brush the border with the melted butter.

Place the tart pan on a baking sheet. Bake the galette for 30 to 35 minutes, or until crust has browned. (Some juices from the fruit will leak onto the baking sheet.) Remove from the oven and let cool on a wire rack for about 5 minutes. Release the sides of the pan. Sprinkle the top of the tart with confectioners' sugar and serve with Crème Fraîche Whipped Cream, if you wish.

NOTE: Reserve the remaining sheet of puff pastry for another use by wrapping well in plastic and storing in the freezer.

Raspberry-Lemon Buttermilk Tart with Candied Lemon Slices

Originally, buttermilk was a by-product of butter churned on a farm, the liquid remaining after the butter was removed from the milk. In medieval Ireland, buttermilk was valued not only as a refreshment, but also as an ingredient used in the production of cheese. Today's buttermilk, however, is a pasteurized milk to which a lactic bacteria culture has been added. In baking it delivers a tangy, yet slightly sweet flavor that complements other ingredients, such as the raspberries in this tart. Top it with the candied lemon slices for an elegant finish. **Serves 8 to 10**

CRUST

1¼ cups all-purpose flour

½ teaspoon salt

2 tablespoons sugar

5 tablespoons cold unsalted Kerrygold Irish butter, cut into small pieces

5 tablespoons cold vegetable shortening, cut into small pieces

3 to 5 tablespoons ice water

FILLING

1½ cups fresh raspberries

½ cup superfine sugar

2 large eggs

¾ cup buttermilk

⅓ cup fresh lemon juice

½ teaspoon grated lemon zest

2 tablespoons all-purpose flour

CANDIED LEMON SLICES

2 cups sugar

2 cups water

1 lemon, thinly sliced

To start the crust: Combine the flour, salt, and sugar in a food processor fitted with a metal blade. Add the butter and shortening and pulse 8 to 12 times, or until the mixture resembles coarse crumbs. Add 3 tablespoons of the water and pulse just until the dough comes together. Add remaining water if necessary. Dust a work surface with flour. Turn out the dough, form it into a ball, then wrap in plastic wrap and refrigerate for 1 hour. Remove the dough from the refrigerator 10 minutes before rolling.

Butter a 10-inch tart pan with a removable bottom. Dust a work surface with flour. Roll out the dough to a circle 12 inches in diameter. Transfer to the prepared pan, fold in the excess dough, and press with your fingers to form thick sides. Refrigerate the crust for 30 minutes, or until firm.

Preheat the oven to 350°F. Prick the bottom and sides of the crust with a fork. Line the crust with foil or parchment paper, fill with pie weights or dry beans, and cover with a pie crust shield (see Note, page 45). Bake for 18 to 20 minutes. Remove the weights, foil, and shield and bake for 12 to 15 minutes more, or until the crust is browned all over. Remove from the oven and let cool on a wire rack. Maintain the oven temperature.

To make the filling: Put the raspberries in the bottom of the tart crust, reserving a few to garnish each serving. Whisk together the superfine sugar, eggs, buttermilk, lemon juice, zest, and flour in a medium bowl. Pour the mixture over the raspberries. Bake the tart for 30 to 35 minutes, or until the filling is barely set. Remove from the oven and transfer to a wire rack to cool completely.

The Claddagh, Galway Bay, Galway

To make the lemon slices: In a medium saucepan over medium heat, combine the sugar and water. Bring to a boil. Add the lemon slices and cook for 1 to 2 minutes, or until the liquid begins to thicken. Remove the pan from the heat and let the lemons and syrup cool completely. With a slotted spoon, remove enough lemon slices from the syrup to arrange decoratively over the top of the tart. Transfer the remaining syrup and slices to a plastic container, cover, and refrigerate for another use for up to 1 week. Release the sides of the pan. Slice the tart, and serve it with the reserved raspberries.

Jameson Chocolate-Walnut-Caramel Tart

In the 200 years since it was first produced, Jameson has become the world's leading Irish whiskey brand. While increasing its global reach, Irish whiskey is making its mark on Irish cookery, especially in desserts, where its distinctive taste complements a wide range of flavors. The combination of whiskey and chocolate is especially delicious, and when nuts and caramel are added, as in this tart, the results are superb. **Serves 8**

CRUST

1¼ cups all-purpose flour

1 teaspoon sugar

¼ teaspoon salt

4 tablespoons cold unsalted Kerrygold Irish butter, cut into small pieces

4 tablespoons cold vegetable shortening, cut into small pieces

2 to 4 tablespoons ice water

CARAMEL SAUCE

¼ cup unsalted Kerrygold Irish butter

½ cup sugar

¼ cup heavy (whipping) cream

FILLING

1 cup walnuts, chopped

½ cup bittersweet (not unsweetened) or semisweet chocolate, broken up into small pieces

¾ cup light corn syrup

½ cup packed light brown sugar

½ cup packed dark brown sugar

4 tablespoons unsalted Kerrygold Irish butter, cut into pieces

3 large eggs

3 tablespoons Jameson Irish whiskey

1 teaspoon vanilla extract

¼ teaspoon salt

Confectioners' sugar for dusting

To start the crust: Combine the flour, sugar, and salt in a food processor fitted with a metal blade. Add the butter and shortening and pulse 8 to 12 times, or until the mixture resembles coarse crumbs. Add 2 tablespoons of the water and process for 15 to 20 seconds, or until the dough comes together. Add the remaining water if necessary and pulse again. Dust a work surface with flour. Turn out the dough, form it into a ball, then wrap it in plastic wrap and refrigerate for 1 hour. Remove the dough from the refrigerator 10 minutes before rolling.

Butter a 10-inch tart pan with a removable bottom. Dust a work surface with flour. Roll out the dough to a circle 12 inches in diameter. Transfer to the prepared pan, fold in the excess dough, and press with your fingers to form thick sides. Freeze for 30 minutes, or until firm.

Preheat the oven to 375°F. Prick the bottom and sides of the crust with a fork. Line the crust with foil, fill with pie weights or dry beans, and cover with a pie crust shield (see Note, page 45). Bake for 18 to 20 minutes. Remove the weights, foil, and shield and bake for 12 to 15 minutes more, or until the crust is browned all over. Remove from the oven and let cool on a wire rack. Maintain the oven temperature.

(continued)

Jameson Chocolate-Walnut-Caramel Tart (continued)

To make the caramel sauce: In a saucepan over medium heat, combine the butter and sugar. Cook, stirring constantly, for 3 to 5 minutes, or until the mixture thickens. Continue cooking until the mixture turns golden brown. Remove from heat and stir in the cream. Pour the caramel mixture into the tart crust, spread evenly over the bottom, and freeze for 15 minutes, or until set.

To make the filling: Sprinkle half of the walnuts and all the chocolate pieces over the caramel. In a large bowl, combine the corn syrup, brown sugars, butter, eggs, whiskey, vanilla, and salt. With an electric mixer, beat until smooth. Pour over the chocolate and walnuts. Sprinkle the remaining half of the walnuts over the top.

Bake the tart for about 50 minutes, or until the filling is nearly set in the center. Remove from the oven and cool on a wire rack for 10 minutes. Release the sides of the pan. Dust the tart with confectioners' sugar, slice, and serve warm.

Plum Tart with Oatmeal Crust

It appears that plum tarts are more popular than ever in Ireland and chefs are inventing new and unusual ways to make them. This recipe, also made tarte Tatin style with the crust cooked on top and the tart flipped over, has an oatmeal crust, a rather clever invention of the Oat Millers of Ireland, an annual promotion organized by Ireland's top oatmeal producers—Flahavan's, Odlums, and Whites Speedicook. Serve it with Crème Fraîche Whipped Cream (page 24). **Serves 8 to 10**

CRUST

1 cup all-purpose flour

½ cup quick-cooking (not instant) Irish oatmeal

6 tablespoons cold unsalted Kerrygold Irish butter

1 tablespoon superfine sugar

1 large egg, beaten

2 tablespoons milk

FILLING

6 to 8 red plums, halved and pitted

⅓ cup brown sugar

3 tablespoons red wine

1 tablespoon milk

2 tablespoons superfine sugar

Crème Fraîche Whipped Cream (page 24)

To start the crust: Combine the flour and oatmeal in a small bowl. With a pastry cutter, 2 knives, or your fingers, cut or rub in the butter until the mixture resembles coarse crumbs. Stir in the superfine sugar. Mix in the beaten egg to make a pliable dough. If it's too dry, add the milk, one tablespoonful at a time. Dust a work surface with flour. Turn out the dough, form it into a ball, then wrap it in plastic wrap and refrigerate for 30 minutes.

To make the filling: Butter a 10-inch quiche pan. Starting in the center of the pan, arrange the fruit, cut side down, in concentric circles. Sprinkle with brown sugar and spoon the red wine over the top.

Preheat the oven to 400°F. Dust a work surface with flour. Roll out the dough to a circle 12 inches in diameter. Place the pastry over the plum mixture, tucking it around the plums at the edge of the pan. Brush with the milk and sprinkle with the superfine sugar. Bake for 20 minutes. Reduce the heat to 350°F and bake for 15 to 18 minutes more, or until golden. Remove the tart from the oven and let cool for 20 minutes on a wire rack. Place a rimmed serving plate over the pan. With potholders to protect your hands, invert the tart onto the plate and remove the pan. Slice the tart and serve warm with the whipped cream.

Apple Tart with Raisin-Nut Topping

At Killeen House, a charming little hotel set in the hills outside Killarney, in County Kerry, proprietors Michael and Geraldine Rosney really know how to make their guests—mostly golfers—feel right at home. The tiny pub in their hotel accepts golf balls from around the world as "legal tender" for a complimentary glass of Guinness, and their restaurant staff is one of the friendliest in the country. Desserts at Killeen House are always a fine complement to the evening meal, including this half-tart, half-crumble, which can be made into a family-size tart or individual tartlets (see Note, page 62), the way it's served in the dining room. It's delicious with vanilla or Cinnamon Ice Cream (page 76). **Serves 8 to 10**

CRUST

1¼ cups all-purpose flour

⅓ cup sugar

Pinch salt

½ cup (1 stick) cold unsalted Kerrygold Irish butter, cut into small pieces

1 large egg yolk

1½ tablespoons milk

FILLING

2 Granny Smith apples, peeled, cored, and cubed

1 Braeburn apple, peeled, cored, and cubed

2 tablespoons sugar

TOPPING

½ cup quick-cooking (not instant) Irish oatmeal, preferably McCann's brand

⅓ cup plus 1 tablespoon self-rising flour

½ teaspoon mixed spice (see Note, page 142)

¼ cup raisins

¼ cup slivered almonds

¾ cup chopped walnuts

2 tablespoons brown sugar

2 tablespoons unsalted Kerrygold Irish butter, melted

To start the crust: Combine the flour, sugar, salt, and butter in a food processor fitted with a metal blade. Pulse 8 to 10 times, or until the mixture resembles coarse crumbs. Add the egg and milk and process for 15 to 20 seconds, or until the dough comes together. Dust a work surface with flour. Turn out the dough, form it into a ball, then wrap in plastic wrap and refrigerate for 1 hour. Remove the dough from the refrigerator 10 minutes before rolling.

Preheat the oven to 350°F. Butter a 10-inch tart pan with a removable bottom. Roll out the dough to a 12-inch circle. Transfer to the prepared pan, fold in the excess dough, and press it to form thick sides.

To make the filling: In a medium bowl, toss the apples with the sugar to coat. Spoon the mixture into the prepared crust.

To make the topping: In a small bowl, combine the oatmeal, flour, mixed spice, raisins, almonds, walnuts, and brown sugar. Stir in the melted butter and blend with a fork. Sprinkle the mixture over the fruit.

(continued)

Apple Tart with Raisin-Nut Topping (continued)

Bake the tart for 30 to 40 minutes, or until the apples are tender and the topping is golden. Remove from the oven and let cool on a wire rack for about 10 minutes. Release the sides of the pan and cut the tart into slices. Serve warm.

NOTE: To make tartlets, butter a 12-cup tartlet pan or a mini-muffin pan with 1$\frac{1}{2}$-inch cups. Roll out the dough, and with a 3-inch cookie cutter, cut out 12 rounds. Press the rounds into the prepared pan. Fill each pastry-lined cup with apple mixture, cover with the topping mixture, and bake for 25 to 30 minutes, or until the apples are tender and the topping is golden. Remove from the oven and let cool on a wire rack for about 10 minutes. Serve warm. **Makes 12 tartlets**

Dingle Peninsula, County Kerry

IRISH WHISKEY: A SHORT HISTORY

Historians claim Irish whiskey was the elixir that cured the sick in the Dark Ages and gave strength to soldiers in the Middle Ages. Artists and writers have called it the nectar that loosens the creativity of playwrights, the voices of singers, and the fingers of musicians. When James Joyce heard "the light music of whiskey falling into a glass," he called it a "most agreeable interlude." Even Russian Czar Peter the Great developed a fondness for Irish and declared, "of all wines, the Irish spirit is the best."

The word "whiskey" is distinctly Irish and comes from the phrase *uisce beatha* (pronounced ishka baahaa), Gaelic for "water of life." The name supposedly came into the English language via soldiers of Henry II who paid several visits to Ireland around 1170. When they arrived to find the natives consuming this *uisce beatha,* they sampled it and liked it immediately, but never learned to pronounce it. Gradually, they anglicized it to "uisce," then to "fuisce," and finally to the word "whiskey" we know today.

Like Scotch whisky (which omits the "e" in its spelling, although Irish whiskey is always spelled with an "e"), Irish is made from water, unmalted barley, and malted barley (the malting occurs when the barley is spread out on a warm floor and allowed to sprout or germinate, before being dried). But unlike Scotch, the barley used for Irish is dried with hot air in closed kilns rather than over an open peat fire. This ensures a honeyed rather than a smoky taste, making it a delicious ingredient in cooking as well as a fine drink. A triple rather than a double distillation (as in Scotch whisky) in giant copper pot stills ensures the maximum purity of Irish, which is stored in oak casks and left to mature, by law, for at least three years, but generally for five to eight years, in cool, dark, aromatic warehouses.

Irish whiskey distilling today takes place in several locations around Ireland producing some of the world's most famous brands of blended and single-malt whiskeys (see Note). In addition to Jameson, which dominates the industry, Bushmills produces three single malts—Bushmills Ten Year Old, Bushmills Twelve Year Old Reserve, and Bushmills Sixteen Year Old Three-Wood—along with some whiskeys that are blended with Irish grain whiskey—Bushmills Original, Black Bush, and Bushmills 1608. Other well-known whiskeys (some of which are only available in Ireland) are Paddy, John Power, Redbreast, and Midleton Very Rare; Tyrconnell, Locke's, Kilbeggan, and Connemara Peated Single Malt, from Cooley's Distillery, in Dundalk, County Louth; Tullamore Dew; and Knappogue Castle Single Malt.

In Ireland, there are five whiskey museum/visitor centers that provide tours and tastings: the Old Jameson Distillery, Bow Street, Dublin; the Jameson Heritage Center, Midleton, County Cork; the Old Bushmills Distillery, Bushmills, County Antrim; Tullamore Dew Heritage Center, Tullamore, County Offaly; and Locke's Distillery Museum, Kilbeggan, County Westmeath. (See Resources, page 163.)

NOTE: Single-malt whiskeys are those that can only be made from malted barley from a single distillery.

Thatched cottage, Adare,
County Limerick

CHAPTER THREE

crumbles and crisps

top: Celtic Apple Crisp, page 74

bottom: Irish Oats, County Meath
(photo courtesy of Odlums Oatmeal Company)

Oats were one of the first cereals cultivated by man. The use of oats for human consumption was well established in Ireland very early in the Christian era, and references to oatmeal can be found in the Great Code of Civil Law compiled in A.D. 438. There is evidence that even before this date, porridge was recognized in Europe as a characteristically Irish food. The temperate, humid climate of Ireland encourages a slow ripening process, which enables the oats to draw the goodness from the soil. The land is irrigated by clean, acid rain–free rivers, and the combination of these factors helps to produce perhaps the finest milling oats in the world. Many are grown in Counties Meath and Kildare. Beyond porridge, you'll find oatmeal used in many Irish dishes, especially in crumbles and crisps, where it provides a nutty flavor and a crunchy texture.

A crumble, perhaps the world's easiest dessert, is created with little more than fresh fruit sweetened with a little sugar, thickened with a little flour, flavored with a little cinnamon, and topped with a crumbly mixture of butter, oatmeal, flour, and sometimes nuts. First cousin to the crumble is the crisp, but the topping in this case is usually bread crumbs and often brown sugar. Similar to both crumbles and crisps are cobblers, deep-dish pies that originated with the Scotch-Irish, I'm told, who added a biscuit or sweet pastry topping to their fruit desserts and "cobbled them up" after the two had been baked together; and buckles, similar to coffeecakes, and so named, supposedly, because of the way the center collapses, or buckles, when it is removed from the oven. Regardless of the name, these fresh fruit desserts are staples in the Irish kitchen and most of the recipes can be adapted to whatever fruit is in season.

Strawberry-Rhubarb Crumble

Strawberries and rhubarb, both of which are harbingers of spring, are one of the most popular Irish fruit and vegetable pairings (yes, botanically rhubarb is a vegetable, although it's treated like a fruit nowadays). Appearing together in pies, jams, syrups, and sauces, strawberry and rhubarb produce a winning sweet-tart taste. Here they are featured in an old-fashioned crumble from Norah Brown, hostess at Grange Lodge, in Dungannon, County Tyrone. For a new twist, Mrs. Brown suggests using Irish digestive biscuits in the topping instead of the more widely used bread crumbs or oatmeal. Serve the crumble with Irish Whiskey Sauce (page 16), if you wish, or vanilla ice cream. **Serves 6 to 8**

FILLING

5 to 6 stalks rhubarb, cut into 1-inch pieces

1 cup fresh strawberries, hulled and sliced

2 tablespoons cornstarch

1 cup sugar

TOPPING

1½ cups all-purpose flour

½ cup brown sugar

½ cup (1 stick) unsalted Kerrygold Irish butter, cut into pieces

⅓ cup crumbled digestive biscuits, such as Carr's or McVitie's brand

Irish Whiskey Sauce (page 16) or vanilla ice cream for serving

Preheat the oven to 350°F. Lightly butter a 9-inch square glass baking pan.

To make the filling: In a large bowl, combine the rhubarb, strawberries, and cornstarch. Stir well to coat the fruit. Transfer to the prepared pan and sprinkle with sugar.

To make the topping: Combine the flour, brown sugar, and butter in a food processor. Pulse 3 to 4 times, or until the mixture resembles coarse crumbs. Transfer to a small bowl and stir in the crumbled biscuits. Sprinkle the topping over the fruit. Bake for 40 to 45 minutes, or until the top is brown and crisp and the fruit is tender. Remove from the oven and serve warm with Irish Whiskey Sauce or vanilla ice cream.

Rhubarb and Ginger Crumble

Originally a small nineteenth-century fishing lodge on the edge of the great Roundstone Bog (150 miles of moorland and lakes), Emlaghmore Lodge, in Ballyconnelly, County Galway, has belonged to the Tinne family for more than seventy-five years. Emlaghmore is comfortably furnished in accordance with its age, and its location between the picturesque fishing village of Roundstone and the golf links course at Ballyconnelly makes it an ideal place to relax and enjoy the wilds of Connemara and delights of its kitchen. Emlaghmore, a member of the Hidden Ireland (see page 29), is under the direction of Nicholas Tinne, creator of this lovely spring crumble. Serve it with vanilla ice cream or Crème Fraîche Whipped Cream (page 24), if you wish. **Serves 6 to 8**

FILLING

5 to 6 stalks rhubarb, cut into 1-inch pieces

¼ cup sugar

1 tablespoon chopped crystallized ginger chips

Grated zest and juice of 1 orange

TOPPING

½ cup (1 stick) unsalted Kerrygold Irish butter, cut into pieces

1½ cups all-purpose flour

2 teaspoons ground ginger

½ cup packed light brown sugar

Vanilla ice cream or Crème Fraîche Whipped Cream (page 24)

Preheat the oven to 375°F. Lightly butter a 9-inch square glass baking pan.

To make the filling: In a medium bowl, combine the rhubarb, sugar, crystallized ginger, orange zest, and orange juice. Stir to combine. Spoon into the prepared pan.

To make the topping: Combine the butter, flour, and ground ginger in a food processor. Pulse 3 to 4 times, or until the mixture resembles coarse crumbs. Stir in the brown sugar. Spread over the fruit mixture. Bake for 40 to 45 minutes, or until the juices are bubbling and the top is crisp. Remove from the oven and serve warm with vanilla ice cream or Crème Fraîche Whipped Cream.

Blackberry-Almond Crumble Cake

Fat blackberries grow in my cousin Kit's garden in Killarney. She picks most of them for making jam, but she also uses some in this delicious cake with a crunchy buttery topping we all find irresistible. Serve this with Irish Mist Whipped Cream, if you wish. **Serves 10 to 12**

TOPPING

2 tablespoons unsalted Kerrygold Irish butter, melted

½ cup packed light brown sugar

½ cup granulated sugar

2 teaspoons ground cinnamon

4 large eggs, beaten

CAKE

1 cup (2 sticks) unsalted Kerrygold Irish butter at room temperature

1 cup granulated sugar

3 large eggs, beaten

¾ cup self-rising flour

Pinch of salt

½ cup milk

1 cup ground almonds

2 cups fresh blackberries

Irish Mist Whipped Cream for serving (optional)

Preheat the oven to 350°F. Butter a 9-inch springform pan and dust with flour. Tap out the excess.

To make the topping: In a small bowl, combine the butter, sugars, and cinnamon. Cool slightly, then stir in the eggs with a fork. Set aside.

To make the cake: Cream the butter and sugar with an electric mixer until light and fluffy. Beat in the eggs. Beat in the flour, salt, and milk. With a wooden spoon, stir until a soft dough forms. Spoon the batter into the prepared pan. Sprinkle the almonds on top, then sprinkle the blackberries over the almonds. Spoon the topping over the blackberries.

Bake the cake for 70 to 75 minutes, or until a skewer inserted in the center comes out clean. Remove from the oven and let cool on a wire rack for 10 minutes. Release the sides of the pan. Slice and serve warm with Irish Mist Whipped Cream, if you like.

Irish Mist Whipped Cream:

1 cup heavy (whipping) cream

1 tablespoon confectioners' sugar

2 tablespoons Irish Mist liqueur

In a chilled bowl, beat the cream and the confectioners' sugar with an electric mixer until soft peaks form. Add the Irish Mist and beat until stiff peaks form. **Makes about 1 cup**

Pear and Ginger Crumble

Desmond and Melanie Sharp Bolster offer their guests at Glenlohane, in Kanturk, County Cork, a relaxed stay in a setting that has remained essentially unchanged after more than two centuries, including some furniture and memorabilia that depict the family's 250 years of residence. Like other members of the Hidden Ireland (see page 29), Glenlohane provides glorious meals with the comforting touch of home cooking. Serve this with Vanilla Bean Whipped Cream (recipe follows), if you wish. **Serves 6 to 8**

FILLING

3 pounds Bartlett or Anjou pears, zested, cored, and sliced

2 tablespoons fresh lemon juice

⅓ cup sugar

2 tablespoons minced crystallized ginger chips

1½ tablespoons all-purpose flour

TOPPING

1 cup all-purpose flour

⅔ cup quick-cooking (not instant) Irish oatmeal, such as McCann's brand

⅔ cup packed light brown sugar

1 teaspoon ground cinnamon

Pinch of salt

½ cup (1 stick) unsalted Kerrygold Irish butter, cut into small pieces

Vanilla Bean Whipped Cream (optional) for serving

Preheat the oven to 375°F. Lightly butter a 13-x-9-x-2-inch glass baking pan.

To make the filling: In a medium bowl, combine the pears and lemon juice. Stir in the sugar, crystallized ginger, and flour. Spoon into the prepared pan.

To make the topping: In a medium bowl, combine the flour, oatmeal, brown sugar, cinnamon, and salt. Add the butter, and stir with a fork until moist clumps form. Sprinkle the topping over the fruit. Bake for 45 to 50 minutes, or until the topping is golden and the pears are tender. Serve warm with the whipped cream, if you like.

Vanilla Bean Whipped Cream:

1 cup heavy (whipping cream)

2 tablespoons sugar

½ vanilla bean, halved lengthwise (see Note, page 14)

In a chilled bowl, beat the cream and sugar with an electric mixer until soft peaks form. Add the seeds from the vanilla bean and beat until stiff peaks form. **Makes about 1 cup**

Blueberry Crumble Cake

Part crumble, part cake, this delicious blueberry dessert is particularly popular during Ireland's blueberry season, which runs from the end of July through mid-September. Due to the big demand for the fruit, however, large berries are picked and frozen in peak condition to provide the juicy, flavorful fruit year-round. Derryvilla Farm in Derryvilla, Portarlington, County Offaly (see page 95), is the country's largest and first commercial blueberry farm. **Serves 10 to 12**

TOPPING

⅓ cup packed light brown sugar

⅓ cup granulated sugar

½ cup chopped walnuts

2 tablespoons unsalted Kerrygold Irish butter

1½ teaspoons ground cinnamon

½ teaspoon ground nutmeg

CAKE

2 cups all-purpose flour

1 cup granulated sugar

1 tablespoon baking powder

½ teaspoon ground nutmeg

½ cup (1 stick) unsalted Kerrygold Irish butter, cut into pieces

1 cup buttermilk

2 large eggs

2 teaspoons vanilla extract

1½ cups fresh blueberries

Preheat the oven to 350°F. Butter a 9-inch square baking pan and dust with flour. Tap out the excess.

To make the topping: In a small bowl, combine the sugars, walnuts, butter, cinnamon, and nutmeg. Set aside.

To make the cake: Combine the flour, sugar, baking powder, and nutmeg in a food processor. Pulse 2 to 3 times to blend. Add the butter and pulse 8 to 10 times, or until the mixture resembles coarse crumbs.

In a large bowl, whisk together the buttermilk, eggs, and vanilla. Add the dry ingredients to the buttermilk mixture and stir to blend. Fold in the blueberries. Spoon the batter into the prepared pan and sprinkle with the topping. Bake for 60 to 65 minutes, or until a skewer inserted into the center comes out clean. Remove from the oven and let cool on a wire rack for 15 minutes. Slice and serve warm.

Celtic Apple Crisp

Apples have always played an important part in Irish folklore, tradition, and diet, so it's no surprise to find apple desserts in great supply and variety. This apple crisp, which is sometimes called "apple crunch" when the apples are first cooked to soften them, is flavored with a respectable dose of Celtic Crossing Liqueur and topped with a combination of white bread crumbs and oatmeal. Flahavan's, Odlums, and McCann's are Ireland's biggest producers of oats, although McCann's is the most widely known in the United States because it started to export in the early part of the twentieth century to cities with large Irish populations, such as New York, Boston, Philadelphia, Detroit, San Francisco, Montreal, and Vancouver. Serve the crisp warm with Cinnamon Ice Cream (page 76), a dessert frequently served at No. 10, a luxurious Dublin townhouse located on the quays of the River Liffey. **Serves 6 to 8**

TOPPING

1 cup fresh white bread crumbs (see Note, page 19)

1 cup quick-cooking (not instant) Irish oatmeal, such as McCann's brand

6 tablespoons unsalted Kerrygold Irish butter, melted

¼ cup packed brown sugar

½ teaspoon ground cinnamon

FILLING

⅓ cup Celtic Crossing Liqueur

⅓ cup water

⅓ cup golden raisins

1 teaspoon vanilla extract

2 ½ pounds Granny Smith or Braeburn apples

⅓ cup sugar

Cinnamon Ice Cream (optional; page 76) for serving

To make the topping: In a small bowl, combine the bread crumbs, oatmeal, butter, brown sugar, and cinnamon. Set aside.

To make the filling: In a small saucepan over medium heat, bring the Celtic Crossing and water to a boil. Add the raisins and vanilla, stir, then remove from heat, cover, and let stand for 1 hour, or until cool.

Preheat the oven to 375°F. Lightly butter an 8-inch square glass baking pan.

Transfer the raisins and their liquid to a large bowl. Peel, core, and slice the apples. Combine the apples and sugar with the raisins. Spoon half of the apples into the prepared dish; top with half the bread crumb–oatmeal mixture. Repeat the layers with the remaining apples and bread crumb–oatmeal mixture. Bake for 50 to 60 minutes, or until the apples are tender and the topping is crisp and browned. Remove from the oven and let cool on a wire rack for 5 minutes. Serve warm with cinnamon ice cream, if you wish.

Cinnamon Ice Cream

½ cup sugar

½ cup water

1 cinnamon stick

2 cups heavy (whipping) cream

¼ teaspoon ground cinnamon

3 large egg yolks

In a small saucepan over medium heat, combine the sugar and water. Bring gently to a boil, and cook for 2 to 3 minutes, or until the sugar is dissolved and the mixture is syrupy. Remove from the heat and let cool.

In another small saucepan over medium heat, combine the cinnamon stick and cream. Bring gently to a boil and cook for 2 to 3 minutes, or until the mixture thickens slightly. Remove the cinnamon stick.

Whisk together the ground cinnamon and egg yolks. Add the sugar syrup and whisk for 3 to 5 minutes, or until the mixture is thick and mousselike. Set the bowl over a dish filled with ice and continue to whisk for 5 to 7 minutes, or until the mixture is cooled. Whisk in the cream.

Process in an ice cream maker according to manufacturer's directions, or freeze in a plastic container until the mixture is half frozen, then whisk again and freeze until firm. **Makes 1½ pints**

THE APPLE FARM

In the late 1960s, the Traas family moved from southwest Holland to Ireland and began growing apples on a tract of land situated between Cahir and Clonmel, in County Tipperary, next to the main Limerick-Waterford road. They had been involved in fruit growing in Holland for years, and they quickly began to establish orchards in their adopted homeland. Today, under the direction of second-generation grower Con Traas, the Apple Farm is planted with a dozen varieties of eating and cooking apples including Discovery, Grieve, Katja, Cox's Pippin, Golden Delicious, Jonagored, and Bramley's, and it has expanded to include plantings of plums, pears, raspberries, and strawberries. The Traas family retails their produce, apple juice, fruit jams, and jellies in their barn shop in Moorstown. They also supply restaurants and hotels with their award-winning fruits. (See Resources, page 163.)

Pear Crisp

This fruit crisp is so incredibly easy to make that it seems too good to be true. Pair it with Cinnamon Ice Cream (page 76) or sweetened whipped cream for the traditional approach, or with Cashel Blue and Cider Ice (see page 42). **Serves 6**

TOPPING

1½ cups all-purpose flour

¼ cup packed light brown sugar

¼ cup granulated sugar

½ cup chopped hazelnuts

½ cup (1 stick) unsalted Kerrygold Irish butter, melted

FILLING

8 Bartlett or Anjou pears, peeled, cored, and sliced

1½ tablespoons ground cinnamon

1 teaspoon ground nutmeg

To make the topping: In a small bowl, combine the flour, sugars, and hazelnuts. Stir in the butter and set aside.

To make the filling: Preheat the oven to 375° F. Butter a 9-inch pie plate. Starting in the center of the plate, arrange the pears in a concentric circle around the plate. Sprinkle with some of the cinnamon and nutmeg.

Continue to layer the pears, sprinkling each layer with cinnamon and nutmeg. Spoon the topping mixture over the pears. Bake for 60 to 75 minutes, or until the topping is crisp and the pears are tender. Remove from the oven and let cool on a wire rack for 5 minutes. Cut into slices and serve warm.

THE STORY OF OATMEAL

Oats were one of the first cereals cultivated by man. They were grown in ancient China as long ago as 7000 B.C. The Greeks are believed to have been the first to make porridge from oats, but the Romans introduced oats to other countries in Western Europe and also gave them other cultivated crops. They named "cereal," after Ceres, the Roman goddess of agriculture.

The cultivation of oats is particularly suited to Ireland's climatic conditions (including fertile soil, a temperate climate, and abundant rainfall), and oatmeal was a staple of the Irish from prehistoric times until the seventeenth century. Vast quantities of oatmeal were consumed in the form of porridge or "stirabout," a thick mixture. Flahavan's, which has been milling Irish oats for over six generations at the factory beside the river Mahon, in County Waterford; and Odlums, founded in 1845 in Portlaoise, in County Laois, are Ireland's largest brands. McCann's, which dates to 1800 and is now a sister company of Odlums, is most well-known in the United States. All three produce several kinds of rolled oats for old-fashioned or quick-cooking oatmeal, as well as steel-cut or pinhead oats. The quality of Irish oats and the distinctive crunchy texture make them perfect for baking. (See Resources, page 163.)

Adare Manor Hotel and Golf Resort,
Adare, County Limerick

CHAPTER FOUR

fools and flummeries

As early as 1746, a recipe for gooseberry fool appeared in the handwritten cookbook of an Irishwoman named Sara Power, who instructed: "Put a quart of Gooseberrys in a bell-mettle skillet, with as much cold water as will cover them, boyle them to mash, then strain them thro' a hair sieve, free from seeds, or skins. Put the pulp in the dish you intend to use, with half a pound of sugar, the yolk of 4 eggs—To serve it, put some Nutmeg and Sack [a sweet wine] in it, remember to beat and mix it well."

Her early recipe for a fruit fool—the word supposedly derives from the French *fouler,* meaning "to crush"—calls for combining puréed fruit with beaten eggs and sugar. Other recipes suggest blending the fruit with whipped cream, sour cream, egg whites, or yogurt for a virtually "foolproof" dessert. The fruit mixture may be sweetened with sugar or honey and enhanced with toasted oatmeal, cream cheese, and, of course, Irish whiskey, to create a flummery or a *cranachan.* Two other old-fashioned desserts that resemble a fool are syllabub and posset, both of which are made with fruit juice rather than puréed fruit. Originally served as drinks, modern recipes for syllabub and posset add whipped cream to transform them into fool-like sweets. As in the old-fashioned crumble and crisp, almost any fruit in season can be adapted to create an updated version of a fool, and a food processor or blender is a great substitute for Miss Power's directions for "boyling them to mash."

Gooseberry Fool

A fool is traditionally made from gooseberries, which produce a lovely color and flavor, although fruit fools are open to all kinds of improvisation. Serve this with Oatmeal Cookies (page 129). **Serves 4**

4 cups fresh or bottled gooseberries (see Note)

½ cup water

½ cup sugar

1¼ cups heavy (whipping) cream

1 teaspoon vanilla extract

Chill four 8- or 9-ounce stemmed glasses. In a medium saucepan over medium-low heat, combine the gooseberries, water, and ¼ cup of the sugar. Cook for 8 to 10 minutes, or until the fruit begins to break up and soften. Press through a fine mesh sieve to remove the seeds. Let cool.

Whip the cream with an electric mixer until soft peaks form. Beat in the remaining ¼ cup of sugar and the vanilla. Fold into the fruit purée. Spoon into the glasses and refrigerate for 1 hour or more, or until firm.

NOTE: Gooseberries are a common ingredient in some German desserts and can be found bottled under the Odenwald label in the foreign foods section of some supermarkets.

Fraughan Fool

According to the renowned Irish cookery writer Theodora FitzGibbon, "next to the apple—the most Irish of all fruits—is the bilberry," a member of the same family as the blackberry and wild blueberry. In Ireland, the bilberry is also known as "fraughan" (pronounced frocken); there are several wild varieties, which grow in bogs, moors, or wherever heather grows. One of the greatest celebrations in the Celtic calendar is Lammas Sunday, also called Fraughan Sunday, observed on the Sunday closest to August 1. As the first fruit to ripen, the fraughans are traditionally picked during the festival of Lughnasa (the Irish word for "August") and eaten in pies, jams, and fools. Cultivated blueberries are much easier to come by and are used in this recipe as a substitute for fraughans. Serve this with Macaroons (page 132). **Serves 4**

½ cup heavy (whipping) cream

½ cup sour cream

2 tablespoons sugar

3 to 4 drops almond extract

2 cups fresh blueberries (reserve a few for garnish)

4 digestive biscuits, such as McVitie's or Carr's brand

¼ cup ground almonds

Chill four 8- or 9-ounce stemmed glasses. Whip the cream with an electric mixer until soft peaks form. Fold in the sour cream, sugar, and almond extract.

In a saucepan over medium-low heat, cook the berries for 8 to 10 minutes, or until they begin to break up and soften.

Remove from the heat and let cool. Spoon 1 to 2 tablespoons of the cooked berries into each of the glasses. Combine the remaining berries with the cream mixture and spoon over the cooked berries. Crumble 1 cookie over each glass and garnish with some of the reserved fresh berries and ground almonds. Serve immediately, or refrigerate until ready to serve.

Apple Fool

Most fruit fools are made from spring and summer berries, so it's a treat to find an autumn recipe that calls for apples, although you might substitute pears. The cloves and sour cream provide an unusual, distinctive flavor and a slightly dense texture. Serve this with Macaroons (page 132). **Serves 4**

---

1 pound Granny Smith apples, peeled, cored, and sliced

Grated zest of ½ lemon

½ teaspoon ground cloves

2 tablespoons water

⅓ cup superfine sugar

2 large eggs, separated (see Note)

½ cup sour cream

Fresh mint sprigs for garnish

Chill four 8- or 9-ounce stemmed glasses. In a small saucepan over medium-low heat, combine the apples, lemon zest, cloves, and water. Cover and simmer for 10 minutes, or until the apples begin to break up and soften. Transfer to a food processor or blender. Process for 10 to 20 seconds, or until the fruit is puréed. Return to the saucepan and stir in the sugar. Add the egg yolks and stir over low heat for 5 minutes, or until thickened. Remove from the heat and let cool for 10 minutes. Stir in the sour cream and refrigerate for 1 hour.

In a medium bowl, beat the egg whites with an electric mixer until stiff, glossy peaks form. Fold into the cold apple purée. Spoon the mixture into the glasses and refrigerate for 1 hour or more, or until slightly firm. Garnish with mint sprigs.

NOTE: If you prefer not to eat raw eggs, you might wish to substitute pasteurized egg products such as All Whites® or Egg Beaters.® If you use one of these products, add 1½ teaspoons of cream of tartar before whipping.

Thatched cottage, Adare, County Limerick

Strawberry Flummery

Flummery is a sweet, soft pudding made of stewed fruit (usually berries) thickened with cornstarch. Old-time flummeries were made by cooking oatmeal until smooth and gelatinlike, then adding milk and either sugar or honey to sweeten. In the eighteenth century, the dish became a gelatin-thickened cream- or milk-based dessert flavored generously with sherry, Madeira, or rum. Modern recipes use toasted oatmeal. Serve this with Shortbread Cookies (page 130). **Serves 4**

²/₃ cup quick-cooking (not instant) Irish oatmeal, preferably McCann's, toasted (see Note)

4 cups fresh strawberries, hulled, plus 4 whole berries for garnish

5 tablespoons sugar

1¼ cups heavy (whipping) cream

²/₃ cup plain yogurt or sour cream

1 tablespoon dark rum

Chill four 8- or 9-ounce stemmed glasses. Set aside 4 teaspoons of the toasted oatmeal for a garnish.

Put the hulled strawberries in a large bowl and mash, or pulse a few times in a food processor. Stir in 1 tablespoon of the sugar.

Whip the cream with an electric mixer until soft peaks form. Fold in the yogurt or sour cream, the remaining 4 tablespoons of sugar, the rum, and oatmeal. Spoon 1 to 2 tablespoons of the strawberries into the bottom of each glass. Spoon 1 to 2 tablespoons of the oatmeal-cream mixture over the berries. Repeat the layers. Refrigerate for at least 1 hour, or until set.

At serving time, sprinkle 1 teaspoon of the reserved oatmeal on top of each glass and garnish with a whole strawberry.

NOTE: To toast oatmeal, spread it out on a baking sheet. Bake at 350°F for 15 minutes, or until toasted, shaking the pan at 5-minute intervals to prevent burning. Remove from the oven and let cool.

Raspberry-Rhubarb Fool

Adare Manor, in Adare, County Limerick, was ranked Number One European Resort in 2003. It is, needless to say, one of Ireland's most luxurious properties. It also boasts one of the country's most ambitious kitchens, with a staff headed by chef Thomas Andrews and his wife, Fidelma, who is in charge of pastries. Together, they prepare five-star meals for the main dining room, as well as more casual meals to a legion of locals and international golfers in the Clubhouse, at the manor's golf course. This old-fashioned fool is part of a more elaborate creation that Fidelma makes at the manor, where she starts with a light ginger sponge, then alternates layers of a tart compote and creamy fool. This is a simplified "fool only" version. Serve it with Macaroons (page 132). **Serves 6**

1½ cups water

1 cup sugar

4 to 5 stalks rhubarb, sliced

1 cup fresh raspberries

One ¼-ounce envelope unflavored gelatin

1 tablespoon fresh lemon juice

3 large egg whites

½ cup heavy (whipping) cream

Chill six 8- or 9-ounce stemmed glasses. In a medium saucepan over medium heat, combine 1 cup of the water and ½ cup of the sugar. Bring to a boil, and cook for 4 to 5 minutes, or until syrupy. Add the rhubarb, reduce the heat, and cook for another 10 to 15 minutes, or until the fruit is tender. Add the raspberries and cook for 2 to 3 minutes longer, or until the fruit begins to break up. Remove the pan from the heat.

In a small saucepan over medium heat, heat the remaining ½ cup of the water. Sprinkle with the gelatin and stir until dissolved. Stir the gelatin mixture and lemon juice into the fruit mixture. Let cool for 20 to 25 minutes, then refrigerate overnight.

In a large bowl, beat the egg whites with an electric mixer until soft peaks form. Add the remaining ½ cup of sugar and beat until stiff peaks form. In another bowl, beat the cream with an electric mixer until soft peaks form. Fold half of the fruit mixture into the cream, then fold in the whites. Spoon some of the remaining fruit mixture into the bottom of each glass. Fill the glasses with the fruit and cream mixture and refrigerate for 1 to 2 hours, or until firm.

Flahavan's Raspberry Flummery

Much like a cranachan or a curach (an Irish honey-and-oatmeal dish), this dessert relies on toasted oatmeal, cream, and fruit, but here the raspberries are left whole. Cream cheese adds a bit of tang, and Irish whiskey provides the kick. Serve this with Oatmeal Cookies (page 129). **Serves 4**

4 tablespoons cream cheese at room temperature

²/₃ cup heavy (whipping) cream

2 tablespoons honey

¹/₃ cup Irish whiskey

¹/₄ cup Flahavan's Irish oatmeal, toasted (see Note, page 87) and cooled

2 cups fresh raspberries (reserve a few for garnish)

Chill four 8- or 9-ounce stemmed glasses. In a medium bowl, combine the cream cheese and cream. Whip with an electric mixer until soft peaks form. Add the honey and whiskey and continue to beat until stiff peaks form. Fold in the toasted oatmeal.

Set aside a few raspberries for garnish. Spoon 1 to 2 tablespoons of the cream mixture into each of the glasses. Spoon 1 to 2 tablespoons of the raspberries over the cream. Repeat the layers. Refrigerate for 1 to 2 hours, or until set. Before serving, top with the reserved fruit.

Baileys Blueberry Mousse

Mousse is a French term meaning "froth" or "foam," and this Baileys Irish Cream-enriched dessert is just that. A cross between a pudding and a fool, it is made with whole fruit instead of crushed blueberries and meringue instead of whipped cream. Serve it with Shortbread Cookies (page 130). **Serves 6**

Grated zest and juice of 1 lemon

1 large egg

5 large egg whites

½ cup Baileys Irish Cream liqueur

1 cup sugar

4 tablespoons unsalted Kerrygold Irish butter

⅛ teaspoon cream of tartar

2 cups fresh blueberries (reserve a few for topping)

Chill six 8- or 9-ounce stemmed glasses. In the top of a double boiler set over simmering water, whisk together the lemon zest and juice, egg, 1 egg white, Baileys Irish Cream, and ¾ cup of the sugar. Cook, stirring continuously, for 12 to 15 minutes, or until the mixture thickens. Remove the double boiler from the heat and stir in the butter. Set the top of the double boiler in a large bowl filled with ice and let the mixture cool, whisking occasionally.

In a small bowl, combine the remaining 4 egg whites and the cream of tartar. Beat with an electric mixer until soft, glossy peaks form. Add the remaining ¼ cup of sugar, a little at a time, and continue to beat until stiff peaks form.

Stir a few spoonfuls of the egg white mixture into the cooled custard mixture to lighten it. Fold in the remaining egg whites and 1½ cups of the blueberries. Spoon into glasses and refrigerate for 1 to 2 hours, or until set. At serving time, garnish with the reserved blueberries.

Lemon Syllabub

Lamenting the decline of rural society in 1745, Mrs. Delaney, the wife of the dean of County Down, wrote, "I am sorry to find people out of character, and that wine and tea should enter where they have no pretence to be and usurp the rural food of the syllabub."

In its original form, syllabub was a thick, frothy drink that was first enjoyed in England and eventually became popular in Ireland, where it was made by beating milk with wine or ale, sugar, spices, and sometimes beaten egg whites. A richer version was made with cream. The name originated in Elizabethan times and is a combination of the words "sille" (a French wine that was used in the mixture) and "bub" (old English slang for "bubbling drink"). Because it's now served more often as a dessert rather than a drink, it's called "solid syllabub" and is made with whipped cream flavored with lemon, brandy, or wine. This recipe from the Irish Dairy Board is a delicious make-ahead dessert. Serve it with Shortbread Cookies (page 130). **Serves 6**

---

3 teaspoons finely grated lemon zest

3 tablespoons fresh lemon juice

3/4 cup dry white wine

3 tablespoons brandy

1/3 cup superfine sugar

2 cups heavy (whipping) cream

Strips of lemon zest or mint leaves (optional) for garnish

In a nonreactive bowl, combine the lemon zest and juice, wine, brandy, and sugar. Stir until the sugar has dissolved. Cover and refrigerate overnight to allow the flavors to infuse.

Chill six 8- or 9-ounce stemmed glasses (martini glasses are ideal). Stir the cream into the lemon juice mixture.

With an electric mixer, beat until soft peaks form. Spoon into glasses and refrigerate for 4 to 6 hours, or until set. Garnish with a strip of lemon zest or some mint leaves, if desired.

Posset Cúchulainn

Close kin to a syllabub is a posset, a drink that originated during the Middle Ages. It was made of hot milk, wine or ale, sugar, and spices. This posset is a dessert named in honor of Cúchulainn, a mythical Irish hero who was closely associated with the area around County Louth. Made with Cooley's (a local Irish whiskey), cream, and orange juice, it was devised by Pat Kerley, chef-proprietor of Quaglino's, in Dundalk. Serve it with Macaroons (page 132). **Serves 4**

Juice of 2 large oranges (about 1 cup)

½ cup superfine sugar

1¾ cups heavy (whipping) cream

Dash of Irish whiskey

Confectioners' sugar for dusting

Chill four 6-ounce stemmed glasses. In a medium saucepan over medium heat, combine the orange juice and superfine sugar. Bring to a boil and cook for 5 to 8 minutes, or until reduced by half. Add the cream and whiskey, return to a boil, then remove from heat and let cool completely. Spoon into the glasses and refrigerate for 8 to 10 hours, or until set. Dust the tops with confectioners' sugar.

DERRYVILLA FARM

The blueberry is a native American fruit and was not introduced into Ireland until the early 1950s. The idea of growing American highbush blueberries was the brainchild of an Irish horticulturist whose research first indicated that the commercial potential of this slow-growing American cousin of the native bilberry or fraughan (see page 83) could be realized in the sunny southeast counties of Wexford and Waterford. However, since the blueberry prefers a peat-enriched soil, the boglands of County Offaly proved to be a better location, and in 1965 a ten-acre plantation was established near Portarlington.

Under the direction of John and Belinda Seager, Derryvilla Farm is Ireland's first commercial and most successful blueberry operation, and has inspired a number of other farmers to plant this delicious and versatile fruit. In addition to supplying the country with some of the finest blueberries, Derryvilla Farm also produces a range of gourmet blueberry products such as blueberry relish, preserve, tonic, and coulis. (See Resources, page 163, and the recipes using blueberries found throughout this book.)

Dingle Peninsula, County Kerry

tea breads and cakes

top: Quay House Tea Brack, page 109

bottom: Garden Art, Castle Ward House, Strangford, County Down

Drinking a cup of tea is one thing; having tea is quite another. Irish cookery writer Monica Sheridan claims that "the great variety of Irish breads owes its existence to the traditional eating habits of the Irish people," and even though tea was always the drink of choice for both breakfast and dinner (a hearty noontime meal in rural Ireland), it was the late afternoon ritual of "tea" that made an Irishwoman extend herself at baking. "It is because of this tradition that so many varieties of bread have evolved in Ireland," says Sheridan.

The formal tradition of "afternoon tea" can be traced back to Anna, the seventh Duchess of Bedford, who is reputed to have introduced the idea in the early 1880s. Too hungry to wait for dinner, she conceived the idea of having tea and snacks served around four or five o'clock in the afternoon. Some time earlier, the Earl of Sandwich had the idea of putting a filling between two slices of bread. So thanks to the duchess and the earl, the combination of tea and sandwiches formed the basis of afternoon tea.

For working and farming communities, afternoon tea became "high tea," a cross between the delicate afternoon meal enjoyed in drawing rooms and tea gardens and the dinner enjoyed in houses of the gentry in the evening. A more substantial affair than afternoon tea, and one that is most common in Irish homes, it can include bacon and eggs, beans, sausages, salads, sandwiches, and potted meats, but it is always accompanied by a variety of home-baked bread, scones, and cakes.

To host your own afternoon tea, start with a selection of savory finger sandwiches like cheddar and tomato or smoked salmon and cucumber on brown bread; and egg salad with watercress or chicken salad with whole-grain mustard on white bread with crusts removed. Offer several varieties of tea—Irish brands like Barry's, Bewleys, or Lyons—along with Assam, Ceylon, orange pekoe, and Earl Grey. Tea should be served in china cups with crisp linens.

Serve tea breads and warm, buttery scones next along with strawberry jam, clotted cream, Lemon Curd (page 134), or Crème Fraîche Whipped Cream (page 24). For the final course, offer a platter of cakes and tartlets, preferably on a tiered serving dish.

Irish Soda Bread

Irish soda bread is, unquestionably, the most favored companion to a cup of tea. Although recipes vary, it's safe to say that all the cake-like soda breads most familiar to Irish-Americans share the same ingredients— flour, sugar, eggs, salt, baking soda, baking powder, and buttermilk. Whether to use butter or oil, dark or golden raisins, and caraway seeds or not, and whether to bake the bread as a round, free-standing loaf on a baking sheet or in a cast-iron skillet or in a loaf pan are open to debate. I've judged two serious soda bread competitions in the past ten years—the most recent one had nearly one hundred entries—and to say that not one was the same is to totally understate the enormous variety. Having said that, I offer only one—this from my mother—which I have grown to love. **Makes 1 loaf**

---

4 cups all-purpose flour

3 tablespoons sugar

1 teaspoon salt

1 teaspoon baking powder

1 teaspoon baking soda

4 tablespoons cold unsalted Kerrygold Irish butter, cut into pieces, plus extra butter for serving

1 large egg, beaten

2 cups buttermilk

1 cup golden raisins

3 tablespoons caraway seeds

1 egg beaten with 1 tablespoon milk or water

Kerrygold Irish butter for serving

Preheat the oven to 425°F. Lightly grease a large baking sheet or cast iron skillet.

Sift the flour, sugar, salt, baking powder, and baking soda into a food processor fitted with a metal blade. Add the butter and pulse 8 to 12 times, or until the mixture resembles coarse crumbs. Add the egg and buttermilk and process for 15 to 20 seconds, or until the dough comes together.

Dust a work surface with flour. Turn out the dough, add the raisins and caraway seeds, and with floured hands, knead gently to form a large round. Transfer to the prepared baking sheet or skillet. Brush the loaf with the egg wash, and with a serrated knife, cut an "X" into the top. Bake for 40 to 45 minutes, or until the top is golden and a skewer inserted into the center comes out clean. (The bread should sound hollow when the bottom is tapped with a knife.) Remove from the oven and let cool on a wire rack for about 15 minutes. Slice and serve warm with butter.

Kinsale Brown Soda Bread

During a recent stay in Kinsale, County Cork, I discovered a deliciously moist version of brown soda bread topped with crunchy sesame seeds. Most unusual, I thought, especially when I learned that the secret to its moist interior was Italian olive oil! After a fair amount of cajoling, Peter Kellett, proprietor of the Baker's Oven, finally shared his recipe, which is among the most popular breads made in his bakery. Two variations of the classic brown bread follow. **Makes 1 loaf**

---

4 cups whole-meal (whole-wheat) flour

½ cup quick-cooking (not instant) Irish oatmeal, such as McCann's brand

¼ cup wheat bran

1 teaspoon baking soda

Pinch of salt

1 tablespoon sugar

¼ cup olive oil

¼ cup canola oil

2 cups buttermilk

2 tablespoons sesame seeds (optional)

Kerrygold Irish butter for serving

Preheat the oven to 400°F. Butter a 9-x-5-x-3-inch loaf pan.

In a large bowl, combine the whole-wheat flour, oatmeal, wheat bran, baking soda, salt, and sugar. Stir until well blended.

In a small bowl, combine the olive oil, canola oil, and buttermilk. Make a well in the center of the dry ingredients and stir in the liquid with a wooden spoon. Continue stirring until a soft dough forms. Knead gently until smooth. Transfer to the prepared pan and smooth out the top with a spoon or rubber spatula dipped in cold water or buttermilk. Sprinkle the top with sesame seeds, if desired. Bake for 50 to 55 minutes, or until a skewer inserted into the center comes out clean. Remove from the oven and let cool on a wire rack in the pan for 10 to 15 minutes. Remove the bread from the pan and slice. Serve warm with butter.

Variations

Glenview House Whole Meal Bread: At Glenview House, a Georgian home in Midleton, County Cork, Beth Sherrard makes this brown bread, measuring the flour and grain by the fistful. In a large bowl, combine 3 fistfuls of coarse whole-meal (whole-wheat) flour, 2 fistfuls of wheat bran, 1 fistful of wheat germ, 2 tablespoons quick-cooking (not instant) oatmeal such as McCann's brand, 1 teaspoon of light brown sugar, 1 teaspoon of salt, and 2 teaspoons of baking soda. Make a well and add 1 egg, beaten, and 2 cups of buttermilk. Mix as described above and bake for 45 to 50 minutes.

Kilmokea Brown Bread: At Kilmokea Country Manor and Gardens, on Great Island, County Wexford, Emma Hewlitt serves this herb-enriched bread for tea and at dinner. In a large bowl combine 2¾ cups coarse whole-meal (whole-wheat) flour, 2 cups all-purpose flour, 2 handfuls oat bran, 1 handful wheat germ, 1 teaspoon baking soda, 1 to 2 tablespoons minced fresh herbs, and 1 to 2 tablespoons each of fennel seeds, poppy seeds, and sesame seeds. Make a well in the center and add 1 tablespoon molasses and 2 cups buttermilk. Mix as described above. Bake for 15 minutes at 400°F, then reduce the heat to 325°F and bake for 35 minutes more.

Cafe on the Quay Scones

It was cold and rainy in Kinvara—not unusual for a March morning in County Galway—and my husband and I really needed a cup of coffee. At the Cafe on the Quay, located in the center of the colorful village, we found what we were looking for along with a bonus—delicious freshly baked scones, thick clotted cream, and pots of fresh fruit jams and marmalades. Proprietor Christina Ryan was responsible for the goodies and was gracious enough to share one of her recipes, adapted here. Serve the scones with Lemon Curd (page 134), Orange Whiskey Marmalade (page 135), or Crème Fraîche (page 24). **Makes 14 to 16 scones**

3 ¾ cups all-purpose flour

1 ½ tablespoons baking powder

½ teaspoon baking soda

½ teaspoon salt

2 tablespoons sugar

6 tablespoons cold unsalted Kerrygold Irish butter, cut into small pieces

1 large egg, beaten

1 ¼ cups plus 2 tablespoons buttermilk

½ cup golden raisins

Preheat the oven to 400°F. Lightly butter a large baking sheet.

Sift the flour, baking powder, baking soda, salt, and sugar into a food processor. Add the butter and pulse 8 to 10 times, or until the mixture resembles coarse crumbs. Add the egg and 1¼ cups of the buttermilk and process for 15 to 20 seconds, or until the dough comes together.

Transfer to a lightly floured work surface and with floured hands, knead in the raisins. Roll out or pat the dough into a 1-inch-thick round. With a 2-inch round biscuit cutter, cut out 6 to 8 rounds, dipping the cutter in flour before each cut. Arrange the scones on the prepared baking sheet, spacing them 1 inch apart. Brush the tops of the scones with the remaining 2 tablespoons buttermilk.

Bake the scones for 20 to 22 minutes, or until golden. Remove from the oven and let cool on a wire rack. While the first batch is baking, gather the scraps, reroll, and cut out more rounds. Bake as described above. Serve warm or at room temperature.

The Quay, Kinvara, County Galway

McCann's Apple Scones

Raisins or currants are the most popular and traditional additions to a batch of scones, but McCann's Oatmeal has come up with a new one—apples—with cinnamon added for more flavor. **Makes 8 scones**

1 cup all-purpose flour

½ cup McCann's quick-cooking (not instant) oatmeal, plus additional for topping

2 teaspoons baking powder

2 teaspoons ground cinnamon

4 tablespoons Kerrygold Irish butter, cut into small pieces

⅓ cup superfine sugar

2 small Granny Smith apples, peeled, cored, and grated

4 tablespoons milk

Kerrygold Irish butter for serving

Preheat the oven to 400°F. Lightly butter a large baking sheet.

In a large bowl, whisk together the flour, oatmeal, baking powder, and cinnamon. With a pastry cutter, 2 knives, or your fingers, cut or work in the butter until it resembles coarse crumbs. Stir in the sugar and grated apple. Add 3 tablespoons of the milk and stir until a soft dough forms.

Dust a work surface with flour. Turn out the dough, and with floured hands, knead gently until the dough comes together. Pat or roll the dough into an 8-inch round. With a serrated knife that has been dipped into flour, score the dough into 8 wedges, but do not cut all the way through. Brush the top with the remaining 1 tablespoon of milk and sprinkle with the additional oatmeal.

Bake the scones for 25 minutes, or until the top is golden and a skewer inserted into one of the wedges comes out clean. Remove from the oven and let cool for 10 minutes before transferring to a wire rack. Cool completely before separating the scones. Separate the scones and serve warm with butter.

A LITTLE HISTORY OF TEA

Tea has been consumed by the Chinese for thousands of years; one early reference to it dates back to 2737 B.C. According to legend, a Chinese emperor named Shen Nung sat under a tree as he boiled water for drinking. A leaf from the *Camellia sinensis* plant fell into the boiling water and gave the emperor his first cup. The first teas grown for export were sent to Britain from China about 300 years ago. Tea trading has long been associated with famous sailing ships, notably the *Cutty Sark,* which raced from China to Britain with the precious commodity.

The tea that was introduced into Irish culture was cultivated in England. As tea grew in popularity in eighteenth-century Ireland, it became fashionable to serve it at social functions. In 1835, Charles Bewley made history when he brought a ship into Dublin from Canton bearing over 2,000 chests of tea. The *Hellas* was to be the first of many ships traveling directly to Dublin from China, thus ending the monopoly held by Britain's East India Trading Company. Tea merchants all over the world were now free to do business on their own, and Charles Bewley was the first merchant who exercised that freedom in Ireland. Bewley's is one of Ireland's most popular brands of tea and its Oriental Café tea rooms (the most popular of which was founded in 1927 at 78 Grafton Street, Dublin) were the first to sell imported teas, coffees, and tea pastries.

Barry's Tea Company was founded in 1901 by James J. Barry, a Cork merchant, who specialized in high-quality teas. Barry's tea, originally sold from a shop on Prince's Street, grew in popularity, and in 1934 it was awarded the Empire Cup for tea blending. Since the mid-1980s, Barry's has become a dominant national brand in a country with the highest per capita tea consumption in the world (the average person

Tea Shop, Inishmore, Aran Islands, County Galway

consumes four cups a day). More than half the tea imported into Ireland now comes from Africa, chiefly Kenya, and Barry's is considered to have pioneered the use of African teas in their blends. The company's Gold Blend is the market leader. Lyons Tea, another of Ireland's large tea companies, started manufacturing tea in Ireland in 1902. Prior to that time, its tea was exported direct from its U.K. parent company, J. Lyons & Co.

According to Bewley's, there is only one correct way to brew a pot of tea, although over the years, many people have attempted to invent and patent complicated methods, from spirit-heated urns to ornate metal tea infusers: "Fill a kettle to the required level with freshly drawn water. Do not reuse boiled water or top up a partly filled kettle. This deoxygenated water does have an adverse effect on brewing. Heat an earthenware or china tea pot (stainless steel pots tend to taint the brew). Use one teaspoonful of loose tea per person plus one for the pot. When using teabags, use one teabag per person. Take the tea pot to the kettle and pour freshly boiling water over the leaves. Let sit for approximately 2 to 3 minutes and stir. Pour the tea through a fine mesh strainer when using loose tea, unless you have put the tea in a metal tea ball."

Lemon-Ginger Scones

Number 5 Fenn's Quay Restaurant, located in the heart of Cork, is one of the city's most popular dining spots. Serving breakfast, lunch, and dinner, proprietors Eilish and Pat O'Leary offer an innovative menu complemented by an extensive wine list. Jazz on Thursdays and desserts such as warm chocolate pudding and spiced ginger cake account for some of the restaurant's loyal following. They usually pair Lemon Curd Cream with diminutive sponge cakes, but here it tops light, lemony scones spiked with crystallized ginger. **Makes 8 scones**

---

2 cups all-purpose flour

¼ cup superfine sugar

2 teaspoons baking powder

Pinch of salt

6 tablespoons cold unsalted Kerrygold Irish butter

½ cup plus 2 tablespoons half-and-half

1 large egg

1 teaspoon vanilla extract

Grated zest of 1 lemon

⅓ cup chopped crystallized ginger chips

1 egg mixed with 1 tablespoon water

Lemon Curd Cream (facing page), for serving

Preheat the oven to 350°F. Lightly butter a large baking sheet.

Combine the flour, sugar, baking powder, and salt in a food processor. Add the butter and pulse 8 to 10 times, or until the mixture resembles coarse crumbs. Add ½ cup of the half-and-half, 1 egg, the vanilla, and zest and process for 15 to 20 seconds, or until the dough comes together. If necessary, add the additional 2 tablespoons of half-and-half.

Transfer to a lightly floured work surface and with floured hands, knead in the crystallized ginger. Pat or roll the dough into an 8-inch round. With a serrated knife that has been dipped into flour, score the dough into 8 wedges, but do not cut all the way through. Arrange the scones on the prepared baking sheet. Brush the tops of the scones with the egg wash.

Bake the scones for 23 to 25 minutes, or until the tops are golden and a skewer inserted into one of the wedges comes out clean. Remove from the oven and let cool for 10 minutes before transferring to a wire rack. Separate the scones and serve warm with Lemon Curd Cream.

Lemon Curd Cream

3 large eggs

1 cup sugar

½ cup (1 stick) unsalted Kerrygold Irish butter, cut into small pieces

1 tablespoon finely grated lemon zest

½ cup fresh lemon juice

2 cups heavy (whipping) cream

Fill the bottom of a double boiler halfway with water and bring to a simmer. Combine the eggs and sugar in the top of the double boiler. Whisk together until frothy. Add the butter, lemon zest, and juice. Set the top of the double boiler over the simmering water. Cook over medium heat, whisking continuously, for 10 to 15 minutes, or until the mixture thickens and resembles whipped cream. Do not let the mixture boil.

In a medium bowl, whip the cream with an electric mixer until soft peaks form. Fold half the cream into the lemon mixture until well blended. Fold in the remaining cream until fully incorporated. Transfer to a bowl and refrigerate for 1 to 2 hours, or until thick. **Makes 3 cups**

Harborside Restaurant, Cobh, County Cork

Quay House Tea Brack

Dating from about 1820, the Quay House is Clifden's (County Galway) oldest building. It was originally a harbormaster's house, but later became a Franciscan monastery, then a convent, and eventually a townhouse hotel owned by the Foyle family, whose ancestors have been entertaining guests in Connemara for nearly a century. Julia Foyle not only offered me her recipe for tea brack, a fruited loaf similar to fruit cake, but also enlisted many of her fellow cooks in the Hidden Ireland group (see page 29) to contribute recipes as well. They appear throughout the cookbook. **Serves 8 to 10**

---

1 pound mixed dried fruit (golden raisins, dates, apricots, cranberries), chopped

2 ounces candied cherries, chopped

¼ cup chopped walnuts

¼ cup chopped pecans

1 teaspoon ground ginger

1 teaspoon mixed spice (see Note, page 142)

1¼ cups cold tea, such as orange pekoe

1 large egg, beaten

1 cup packed light brown sugar

2 cups self-rising flour

Kerrygold Irish butter for serving

In a large bowl, combine the fruit, nuts, spices, and tea. Let soak for 3 hours, or until the tea is absorbed.

Preheat the oven to 350°F. Butter a 9-x-5-x-3-inch loaf pan.

Stir the egg, sugar, and flour into the fruit mixture and mix until well combined. Pour into the prepared pan and bake for 60 to 75 minutes, or until the top is golden and a skewer inserted into the center comes out clean.

Remove the bread from the oven and cool in the pan on a wire rack for 5 minutes. Turn out onto the rack and cool completely before slicing. Serve with butter.

Wexford Strawberry Tea Loaf

Strawberries are the most popular soft fruit eaten in Ireland, and in the sunny southeastern counties of Wicklow and Wexford, strawberry season arrives in late June or early July. You can buy them at roadside stands, markets, or the many fairs and festivals that celebrate the local crop, like the one at Enniscorthy, in the heart of Wexford, which runs for more than a week. This tea bread is a delicious reminder of the season. **Serves 8 to 10**

1½ cups all-purpose flour

½ teaspoon baking soda

½ teaspoon salt

1 teaspoon ground cinnamon

1 cup sugar

2 large eggs, beaten

½ cup canola oil

1 cup fresh strawberries, hulled and quartered

½ cup chopped walnuts

Preheat the oven to 350°F. Butter a 9-x-5-x-3-inch loaf pan.

In a large bowl, whisk together the flour, baking soda, salt, cinnamon, and sugar. Add the eggs and oil and mix well. Stir in the strawberries and nuts.

Spoon the batter into the prepared pan. Bake the bread for 55 to 60 minutes, or until the top is brown and a skewer inserted into the center comes out clean. Remove from the oven and let cool in the pan on a wire rack for 10 minutes. Turn out onto the rack and cool completely before slicing.

Kilnagrange Apple-Oat Upside-Down Cake

Flahavan's has been milling Irish oats for over six generations at its Kilnagrange Mills in Kilmacthomas, County Waterford. Ever watchful of trends in diet and taste, Flahavan's is also involved with recipe development and has devised a number of delicious recipes easily adaptable to an international audience. This one, a contemporary take on an old-fashioned upside-down cake, features a light-as-air batter that sits atop sliced apples. Its not-too-sweet taste makes it perfect for tea or brunch. **Serves 6 to 8**

¾ cup Flahavan's quick-cooking (not instant) Irish oatmeal

¾ cup warm apple juice

2 tablespoons canola oil

2 large egg whites, lightly beaten

2 teaspoons vanilla extract

1 tablespoon unsalted Kerrygold Irish butter, melted

1 cup packed light brown sugar

1 large Granny Smith apple, peeled, cored, and thinly sliced

Lemon juice for sprinkling

1¼ cups all-purpose flour

1 teaspoon baking soda

1 teaspoon ground cinnamon

½ teaspoon salt

¼ teaspoon ground nutmeg

In a small bowl, combine the oatmeal, apple juice, and oil. Let stand for 10 minutes, or until the liquid is absorbed. Stir in the egg whites and vanilla.

Preheat the oven to 350°F. Butter a 9-inch round baking pan and drizzle with the melted butter. Sprinkle with ¼ cup of the sugar. Starting in the center, arrange the apple slices in overlapping concentric circles around the pan. Sprinkle with a little lemon juice to prevent discoloring. Set aside.

In a large bowl, whisk together the flour, remaining ¾ cup of sugar, the baking soda, cinnamon, salt, and nutmeg. Whisk in the oatmeal mixture until well combined. Pour the batter into the prepared pan.

Bake the cake for 40 minutes, or until the top is golden and a skewer inserted into the center comes out clean. Remove from the oven and let cool in the pan for 10 minutes. Place a rimmed plate on top of the cake, and with potholders to protect your hands, invert the pan onto the plate. Cut into wedges and serve warm.

Scots-Irish Oat Cake

No matter how you slice it—or what you name it— this spicy oatmeal cake is a must for tea. A friend from Northern Ireland calls a version of it "Scots-Irish cake," another from Galway simply calls it "oat cake," and the folks at Flahavan's, the County Waterford oatmeal company, call it "lazy daisy oatmeal cake." Try it with a decadent brown sugar, pecan, and coconut topping, or serve it plain with a sweet-tart strawberry-rhubarb compote (page 28). **Serves 8 to 10**

CAKE

1 cup Flahavan's quick-cooking (not instant) Irish oatmeal

1¼ cups boiling water

1½ cups all-purpose flour

1 teaspoon baking soda

¾ teaspoon ground cinnamon

¼ teaspoon ground nutmeg

½ cup (1 stick) unsalted Kerrygold Irish butter at room temperature

1¼ cups packed light brown sugar

2 large eggs

1 teaspoon vanilla extract

TOPPING

4 tablespoons unsalted Kerrygold Irish butter, melted

½ cup packed light brown sugar

¼ cup heavy (whipping) cream

¾ cup unsweetened flaked coconut

½ cup chopped pecans

To make the cake: Preheat the oven to 350°F. Butter an 8- or 9-inch round baking pan. Dust with flour and tap out the excess. In a small bowl, combine the oats and water. Let soak for 20 minutes. Sift together the flour, baking soda, cinnamon, and nutmeg in a medium bowl.

In a large bowl, cream the butter and sugar together with an electric mixer. Add the eggs and beat until light and fluffy. Stir in the vanilla and oats. Stir the dry ingredients into the oat mixture. Pour into the prepared pan. Bake the cake for 40 to 45 minutes, or until a skewer inserted into the center comes out clean. Remove from the oven and let the cake cool in the pan on a wire rack for about 30 minutes. Invert the cake onto the rack, then turn right side up and place it on an oven-proof cake plate. Spread the cake with the topping.

To make the topping: Preheat the broiler. Combine the butter, sugar, cream, coconut, and pecans in a medium bowl. Spread the topping mixture evenly over the cake and place under the broiler, on the middle rack, for 2 to 3 minutes, or until the top is bubbling. Serve warm or at room temperature.

Victoria Sponge with Lemon Curd and Cream

Another perfect-for-tea cake, this rich layer cake is from Cookery Corner, a collection of recipes devised by Odlums, a flour and oatmeal company with locations in Dublin, Laois, Cork, and Kildare. The filling is a layer of lemon curd topped with whipped cream. If you prefer, replace it with Lemon Curd Cream (page 107). The cake is also delicious spread with 1 cup of strawberry or raspberry preserves, such as Morley's or Folláin (see Resources, page 163), instead of the lemon filling. **Serves 8**

CAKE

1 cup (2 sticks) unsalted Kerrygold Irish butter at room temperature

2 cups superfine sugar

4 large eggs, beaten

2 cups self-rising flour

FILLING

1¼ cups heavy (whipping) cream

6 tablespoons Lemon Curd (page 134)

Confectioners' sugar for dusting

To make the cake: Preheat the oven to 350°F. Butter two 8-inch round cake pans. Line each with parchment or waxed paper. In a large bowl, cream the butter and superfine sugar with an electric mixer until light and fluffy. Beat in the eggs, one at a time, until the mixture is smooth. Sift the flour over the mixture and fold in with a rubber spatula until well combined. Spoon the batter into the prepared pans and smooth the tops.

Bake the cakes for 25 to 30 minutes, or until the tops are golden. Remove from the oven and let cool in the pans on wire racks for 5 minutes. Invert and peel away the paper. Turn right side up and let cakes cool completely on wire racks.

To make the filling: In a small bowl, whip the cream with an electric mixer until soft peaks form. Put the bottom layer of the cake on a serving plate, spread with the Lemon Curd, then with the whipped cream. Carefully place the other layer on top of the whipped cream. Dust the top with confectioners' sugar. Slice and serve immediately.

Martinstown Orange Sponge Cake

This unusual little cake comes by way of Martinstown House, in County Kildare, a country house that was originally part of the extensive estates of the Dukes of Leinster. Hostess Meryl Long told me the cake was traditionally served at tennis parties, a social activity she enjoyed in Kildare in the 1950s. Now she entertains visitors in her charming home, complete with a walled garden, croquet lawn, cattle, sheep, a donkey, and "proper free-range hens." Martinstown House is a member of the Hidden Ireland (see page 29). **Serves 6 to 8**

CAKE

4 large eggs

¼ teaspoon vanilla extract

½ cup sugar

1 cup self-rising flour, sifted

FILLING

1¼ cups confectioners' sugar

Grated zest and juice of 1 orange (about ⅓ cup of juice)

Crème Fraîche (optional, page 24) for topping

Orange segments (optional) for garnish

To make the cake: Preheat the oven to 375°F. Butter a 7-inch round cake pan. Line with parchment or waxed paper. In a large bowl, cream the eggs, vanilla, and sugar with an electric mixer for 3 to 4 minutes, or until light and fluffy. Gently fold the flour into the mixture, ¼ cup at a time, until well combined. Spoon the batter into the prepared pan.

Bake the cake for 18 to 20 minutes, or until the cake springs back when touched lightly in the center. Remove from the oven and let the cake cool in the pan on a wire rack for 10 minutes. Invert onto the rack, peel away the paper, then turn right side up. Cool completely. With a serrated knife, split the cake in half horizontally. Place the bottom layer, cut side up, on a serving plate.

To make the filling: In a small saucepan over medium heat, combine the confectioners' sugar, orange zest, and orange juice. Heat for 4 to 5 minutes, or until the mixture is smooth. Do not boil. Brush the bottom cake layer with 2 to 3 tablespoons of the filling, replace the top, then brush or spread the remaining filling over the top of the cake. Slice and serve with Crème Fraîche, if you wish, and a few orange segments.

Ballynahinch Castle Hotel, Recess
Connemara, County Galway

Simnel Cake

Simnel cake is a rich fruit cake with a center and top layer of marzipan (see Note). It might have been introduced into Ireland by the Anglo-Norman settlers in the twelfth or thirteenth century, although the custom of preparing an enriched wheaten cake for Mothering Sunday, the fourth Sunday in Lent, must have been introduced into Ireland by the Elizabethan settlers in the sixteenth and seventeenth centuries. Tradition suggests that many apprentices and those in domestic service worked and lived away from home. On Mothering Sunday, the original Mother's Day, they could have the day off and were encouraged to go home to visit their mothers. This was known as "going-a-mothering," and a special "mothering cake" was brought along to provide a festive touch. If the workers couldn't go home, they liked to send the cake at Easter, but it had to be one that was sturdy enough to be sent by post. The simnel cake proved to be perfect for such a gift, and it has come to be something of an Easter tradition in Ireland. It is usually decorated with thirteen marzipan balls—representing Jesus and the twelve apostles—which are placed around the edges of the cake. In Ireland, Mothering Sunday is celebrated on the third Sunday of March, roughly equivalent to the original fourth Sunday of Lent. Simnel cake is lovely to serve at tea, and much like the traditional Christmas cake, it keeps well in an airtight container. **Serves 10 to 12**

MARZIPAN

2 cups almonds, finely ground in a food processor

½ cup light brown sugar

1 tablespoon cornstarch plus extra for rolling

1 large egg white, beaten

CAKE

1 cup golden raisins

1 cup dark raisins

1 cup currants

½ cup hot tea

2 tablespoons corn syrup

1 cup all-purpose flour

½ cup self-rising flour

½ cup (1 stick) unsalted Kerrygold Irish butter at room temperature

½ cup light brown sugar

2 large eggs, beaten

2 tablespoons apricot jam

Confectioners' sugar for dusting

To make the marzipan: In a small bowl, combine the almonds, brown sugar, and cornstarch. Add the egg white and stir until the mixture resembles a smooth paste. Roll the marzipan into a ball, wrap it in plastic wrap, and refrigerate for at least 30 minutes, or until firm.

To make the cake: Preheat the oven to 350°F. Lightly butter the bottom and sides of a deep 7-inch round cake pan or springform pan. Line the bottom with waxed or parchment paper and line the sides with a second piece of the paper. In a large bowl, combine the raisins and currants. Pour the tea over the fruit and let it sit for

5 minutes. Stir in the corn syrup. Sift together the flours in a small bowl.

In a large bowl, cream the butter and sugar with an electric mixer until light and fluffy. Add the eggs, one at a time, then stir in the flours until smooth. Stir in the dried fruits and their liquid. Spoon half of the batter into the prepared pan and smooth the top with a rubber spatula. Unwrap the marzipan. Dust a work surface with cornstarch, and roll out one third of the marzipan to a 6-inch circle about $\frac{1}{4}$ inch thick. Lift and gently place it on top of the batter. Spoon the remaining batter on top and smooth again. Rewrap and return the remaining marzipan to the refrigerator. Cover the cake pan tightly with aluminum foil.

Bake the cake for 50 minutes, remove the foil, and bake for 45 to 50 minutes longer, or until a skewer inserted into the center comes out clean. Remove from the oven and let cool completely on a wire rack. Invert the cake onto a baking pan, remove the paper, then turn the cake right side up.

Preheat the broiler (unless you prefer to use a kitchen blowtorch to brown the cake). Put the remaining marzipan on the work surface and roll into a 7-inch round about $\frac{1}{4}$ inch thick. Trim to make the edges smooth. In a small saucepan over medium heat, or in a microwave oven, heat the apricot jam until runny. Brush the jam over the surface of the cake, then press the marzipan firmly on top. Place the cake under the broiler 4 inches from the heat source and broil until the top is lightly browned, or with a kitchen blowtorch, move the flame constantly over the surface until the top browns. Let cool completely. (The cake can be wrapped in plastic wrap and stored in an airtight container for up to 3 weeks, or frozen for 1 month.) To serve, dust the top with confectioners' sugar.

NOTE: Premade marzipan is available in 7-ounce tubes from Odense (see Resources, page 163). Roll out half the marzipan for the center and half for the top.

Gooseberry-Mead Swiss Roll

Gooseberries are one of Ireland's most underused but easily grown cottage garden fruits. Mead, bottled in County Clare under the brand name of Bunratty Meade (see Resources, page 163), is a sweet, honey-based wine popular in Ireland since the days of the Irish chieftains. Together they're a delicious combination in this tea cake/Swiss roll created by chef Freda Wolfe, who works as a restaurant consultant in Dublin. **Serves 8 to 10**

CAKE

¾ cup all-purpose flour

1 teaspoon baking powder

¼ teaspoon salt

3 large eggs

1 cup superfine sugar

⅓ cup water

½ teaspoon vanilla extract

Confectioners' sugar for dusting

FILLING

1 cup fresh or bottled gooseberries (see Note, page 82), drained

¼ cup sugar

1 tablespoon water

3 tablespoons Bunratty Meade

⅔ cup heavy (whipping) cream

Confectioners' sugar for dusting

To make the cake: Preheat the oven to 375°F. Line a 15-x-10-x-1-inch jelly roll pan with waxed paper. Spray the waxed paper with cooking oil spray. In a small bowl, sift together the flour, baking powder, and salt. In a large bowl, cream the eggs and superfine sugar with an electric mixer for about 5 minutes, or until thick and lemon colored. Beat in the water and vanilla, and then the flour mixture. Pour the batter into the prepared pan. Smooth the top with a spatula, spreading the batter to the corners.

Bake the cake for 12 to 15 minutes, or until golden and the center springs back when lightly touched. Remove from the oven and invert the pan onto a clean kitchen towel that has been dusted with confectioners' sugar. Gently peel off the waxed paper and dust the cake with confectioners' sugar. Starting from a short side, gently roll up the cake with the towel. Place, seam side down, on a wire rack, and let cool for 30 minutes or longer while you prepare the filling.

To make the filling: In a small saucepan over medium heat, combine the gooseberries, sugar, and water. Cook for 5 to 7 minutes, or until the gooseberries begin to break up. Remove from the heat and let cool. Transfer to a food processor and pulse 1 to 2 times to roughly purée. Transfer to a small bowl, stir in 1 tablespoon of the mead, and refrigerate for 20 minutes.

In another small bowl, whip the cream with an electric mixer until soft peaks form. Fold into the gooseberry purée. Unroll the cake and remove the towel. Spread with the filling, leaving about a ¼-inch border, and carefully reroll the cake. Cover with plastic wrap and refrigerate for at least 2 hours.

To serve, drizzle the remaining 2 tablespoons of mead over the top of the cake, dust with confectioners' sugar, and slice.

Irish Cream Cheesecake

One of the most popular desserts worldwide is cheesecake. The classic dessert started life well over a century ago in Poland and Russia, where it was traditionally known as "curd cake." The ingredients were based on curd-type cheeses, usually homemade, which were flavored with sugar and baked in a crust of biscuit crumbs or short crust pastry. The modern version is a dreamy blend of cheese—most often cream cheese—sugar, eggs, and any number of flavorings, ranging from lemon juice to white chocolate to Irish cream liqueur. Fresh fruit and tart fruit sauces are perfect partners to the rich Irish cream-enhanced cheese filling in this recipe. If you like, serve it with mixed fresh berries, Blueberry Sauce (page 17), or strawberry-rhubarb compote (see page 53). **Serves 10 to 12**

CRUST

1 cup crumbs from Irish digestive biscuits or wheat biscuits, such as Carr's or McVitie's brand (6 to 8 biscuits)

3 tablespoons sugar

3 tablespoons unsalted Kerrygold Irish butter, melted

FILLING

Three 8-ounce packages cream cheese at room temperature

1 cup sugar

2 teaspoons vanilla extract

1 cup sour cream

1/3 cup Irish cream liqueur, such as Baileys

4 large eggs

TOPPING

1 cup sour cream

1/4 cup sugar

To make the crust: Preheat the oven to 350°F. In a small bowl, combine the crumbs, sugar, and melted butter. Press the crumb mixture onto the bottom and up the sides of a 9-inch round springform pan. Bake for 8 to 10 minutes, or until lightly browned. Remove from the oven and let cool on a wire rack. Maintain the oven temperature.

To make the filling: Combine the cream cheese, sugar, and vanilla in a food processor. Process for 10 to 20 seconds, or until smooth. Add the sour cream and Irish cream liqueur, and process for 5 to 10 seconds. Add the eggs, one at a time, processing after each addition.

Pour the filling over the biscuit crust. Bake the cheesecake for 45 to 50 minutes, or until the edges are puffed and the center is firm. Remove from the oven and let cool on a wire rack for 10 minutes.

To make the topping: In a small bowl, whisk together the sour cream and sugar. Spoon over the warm cheesecake and bake for 10 minutes. Remove from the oven and let cool completely on a wire rack. Cover and refrigerate overnight. Release the pan sides, slice the cheesecake, and serve.

Old Postal Box, Kinsale, County Cork

Rhubarb Cheesecake with Strawberry-Orange Compote

Rhubarb shows up in many traditional Irish desserts, so it's not too much of a stretch to find it in a contemporary recipe such as cheesecake. What sets apart this dessert, from chef Shirley Forde of the Trident Hotel, in Kinsale, County Cork, is the use of champagne and blood oranges (sweet, thin-skinned, red-fleshed oranges) in combination with the rhubarb and strawberries. Desserts don't get more colorful than this! Serves 10 to 12

CRUST

1 cup crumbs from Irish digestive biscuit crumbs or wheat biscuits, such as Carr's or McVitie's brand (6 to 8 biscuits)

3 tablespoons unsalted Kerrygold Irish butter, melted

FILLING

5 to 6 stalks rhubarb, finely chopped

2 tablespoons water

½ cup plus 2 tablespoons superfine sugar

One ¼-ounce envelope unflavored gelatin

1 cup boiling water

Two 8-ounce packages cream cheese at room temperature

¼ cup champagne

2 cups heavy (whipping) cream

TOPPING

5 to 6 stalks rhubarb, finely chopped

2 tablespoons water

1 to 2 tablespoons sugar

One ¼-ounce envelope unflavored gelatin

STRAWBERRY-ORANGE COMPOTE

Juice of 4 blood oranges (about 1 cup)

½ cup sugar

12 fresh strawberries, hulled and quartered

Fresh mint leaves (optional) for garnish

To make the crust: Preheat the oven to 350°F. In a small bowl, combine the crumbs and melted butter. Press the crumb mixture onto the bottom and up the sides of a 9-inch round springform pan. Bake for 8 to 10 minutes, or until lightly browned. Remove from the oven and let cool on a wire rack.

To make the filling: In a small saucepan over medium heat, combine the rhubarb, water, and 2 tablespoons of the superfine sugar. Cook for 4 to 6 minutes, or until the fruit is tender. Transfer to a colander to drain and let cool.

In a small bowl, combine the gelatin and the remaining ½ cup of sugar. Add the boiling water and stir until the

gelatin is completely dissolved, about 5 minutes. In a large bowl, beat the cream cheese with an electric mixer until smooth. Slowly beat in the gelatin mixture. Stir the rhubarb mixture and champagne into the cream cheese mixture. In a medium bowl, whip the cream with an electric mixer until soft peaks form. Fold the cream into the rhubarb-cheese mixture and pour over the biscuit crust. Refrigerate for 3 to 4 hours, or until firm.

To make the topping: In a small saucepan over medium heat, combine the rhubarb and water. Bring to a gentle boil, adding sugar to taste, and cook for 4 to 6 minutes, or until the fruit is tender. Sprinkle in the gelatin and stir for 1 to 2 minutes, or until the gelatin is nearly dissolved. Let cool. When cooled and thickened, spread over the top of the cheesecake. Refrigerate while making the compote.

To make the compote: In a small saucepan over medium heat, combine the juice and sugar. Bring to a gentle boil, and cook, stirring frequently, for 5 to 7 minutes, or until reduced by half. Stir in the strawberries. Cook for 2 to 3 minutes more, or until the sauce is warm.

To serve, cut the cheesecake into slices and serve with the compote drizzled around the base. Garnish with fresh mint leaves, if desired.

Variation

Apple Cheesecake: Con Traas of the Apple Farm makes cheesecake with apples. Make the crust. For the filling, substitute 8 ounces of Bramley's apples, peeled, cored, and sliced, for the rhubarb. Substitute $\frac{1}{4}$ cup apple juice or cider for the champagne. Combine the apples, water, and 2 tablespoons of the superfine sugar in a saucepan and cook for 4 to 6 minutes, or until the apples are tender. Mash and let cool, and proceed with the recipe for the filling. (Omit the topping and compote.)

Chocolate Cheesecake

Ballinkeele House, built in 1840, is the ancestral home of the Maher family. Its present owners are John and Margaret Maher, who have the pleasure of maintaining its glorious past while entertaining and hosting contemporary guests. The house is set in 350 acres of parkland, lakes, and ponds in the lovely village of Ballymurn, in County Wexford. Margaret is a member of Euro-Toques, an association of European chefs dedicated to preserving the quality of regional foods, and she utilizes local ingredients from the family farm and garden to great effect. Though not made from on-site ingredients, her chocolate cheesecake is one of her guests' favorite desserts. When Wexford strawberries are in season, she serves a few alongside each slice of cake. Ballinkeele House is a member of the Hidden Ireland (see page 29). **Serves 8 to 10**

CRUST

1 cup crumbs from 6 to 8 biscuits Irish digestive biscuit, or wheat biscuits, such as Carr's or McVitie's brand

3 tablespoons sugar

3 tablespoons unsalted Kerrygold Irish butter, melted

FILLING

One ½-ounce envelope unflavored gelatin

3 tablespoons water

5 ounces best-quality unsweetened (not bittersweet) chocolate

2 large eggs, separated

One 8-ounce package cream cheese

1 cup sugar

½ cup heavy (whipping) cream

To make the crust: Preheat the oven to 350°F. In a small bowl, combine the crumbs, sugar, and melted butter. Press the crumb mixture onto the bottom and up the sides of a 9-inch round springform pan. Bake for 8 to 10 minutes, or until lightly browned. Remove from the oven and let cool on a wire rack.

To make the filling: In a small bowl, combine the gelatin with 2 tablespoons of the water. Set aside. In a small saucepan over medium-low heat, melt the chocolate with the remaining 1 tablespoon of water. Stir in the egg yolks until smooth.

In a medium bowl, beat the cream cheese and sugar with an electric mixer until smooth. Beat in the chocolate mixture. Slowly drizzle the softened gelatin mixture into the cream cheese and chocolate mixture.

In a small bowl, beat the egg whites with an electric mixer until soft peaks form. In a bowl large enough to hold all the ingredients, whip the cream with an electric mixer until stiff peaks form. Slowly add the cream cheese and chocolate mixture to the whipped cream, then gently fold in the egg whites. Pour into the crust and refrigerate for 3 to 4 hours, or until firm.

Warm Chocolate Cake with Grand Marnier

One of County Kilkenny's most unique accommodations is Waterside, a restored and converted cornstore on the banks of the River Barrow at the Quay in Graiguenamanagh. Dating from 1871, the building is now both a guest house and restaurant under the direction of Brian and Brigid Roberts, who take a friendly and relaxed approach to both endeavors. Brigid's simple chocolate cake, which she spikes with a bit of Grand Marnier, is a perfect example. She serves it warm with homemade vanilla ice cream, but it would also be delicious with Cinnamon Ice Cream (page 76) or Crème Fraîche Whipped Cream (page 24) and a few fresh berries. **Serves 8 to 10**

---

12 ounces milk chocolate

½ cup (1 stick) unsalted Kerrygold Irish butter

4 large eggs

½ cup superfine sugar

½ cup heavy (whipping) cream

2 tablespoons Grand Marnier

Preheat the oven to 350°F. Butter a 10-inch springform pan and line the bottom with waxed or parchment paper.

In a small saucepan over medium-low heat, combine the chocolate and butter. Melt, stirring constantly, until smooth.

In a medium bowl, whisk together the eggs and sugar until thick. Whisk the chocolate, cream, and Grand Marnier into the egg mixture until well blended. Pour into prepared pan. Bake for 30 to 35 minutes, or until a skewer inserted into the center comes out clean. Remove from the oven and let cool in the pan on a wire rack for 15 minutes. Release the sides of the pan. Transfer to a serving plate and cut into slices. Serve warm.

Dark Chocolate Brownies with
White Chocolate Cream and Mixed Berry Coulis

Roly's Bistro, located in the fashionable suburb of Ballsbridge, is one of Dublin's most popular bistro-style restaurants. Since opening night in 1992, Colin O'Daly has served as chef-patron, overseeing an "haute cuisine menu with ready-to-wear prices." He was recently invited to devise a sixty-minute dinner party menu for Dublin's Food & Wine *magazine and offered this easy-to-assemble decadent dessert.* **Serves 8 to 9**

BROWNIES	WHITE CHOCOLATE CREAM	BERRY COULIS
½ cup self-rising flour	1¼ cups heavy (whipping) cream	½ cup fresh orange juice
¼ cup cocoa	2 teaspoons confectioners' sugar	¼ cup water
2 large eggs	3 egg yolks	2 tablespoons superfine sugar
1 cup superfine sugar	¾ cup white chocolate chips	½ cinnamon stick
½ cup (1 stick) unsalted Kerrygold Irish butter, melted	2 tablespoons Celtic Crossing Liqueur	1 cup mixed fresh or thawed frozen berries (strawberries, raspberries, blackberries), with a few reserved for garnish
1 tablespoon vanilla extract		
1 tablespoon semisweet chocolate chips		

To make the brownies: Preheat the oven to 300°F. Line an 8-inch square baking pan with waxed paper and butter the paper. In a small bowl, sift together the flour and cocoa. In a large bowl, beat the eggs and sugar with an electric mixer until light and fluffy. Beat in the butter. Stir in the dry ingredients, vanilla, and chocolate chips. Spoon the batter into the prepared pan. Bake the brownies for 30 to 35 minutes, or until a skewer inserted into the center comes out clean. Remove from the oven and let cool completely in the pan on a wire rack.

To make the cream: In a small bowl, beat the cream and confectioners' sugar with an electric mixer until soft peaks form. Set aside. Place a small heat-proof bowl over a saucepan of boiling water. Put the egg yolks in the bowl and whisk for 2 to 3 minutes, or until they start to thicken. Remove from the heat, and with an electric mixer, beat until the eggs are light and fluffy.

In a small saucepan over low heat, combine the white chocolate chips and Celtic Crossing. Melt the chocolate, stirring constantly, for 5 to 8 minutes, or until smooth. Whisk the chocolate mixture into the eggs, then fold in the cream mixture.

To make the coulis: In a medium saucepan over medium heat, combine the orange juice, water, superfine sugar, and cinnamon stick. Bring to a boil, stir in the berries, then reduce the heat to low and simmer for 3 to 5 minutes, or until the berries are soft and warm. Remove the cinnamon stick and let cool thoroughly.

To serve, cut the brownies into squares and place on dessert plates. Spoon some of the berry coulis over each, and place a spoonful of the cream next to it. Garnish with a few of the reserved berries.

Jam Tarts

These little tarts are a version of the classic Bakewell tart, an almond cream–filled pastry that sports a layer of raspberry jam on the bottom crust. **Makes 24 tartlets**

PASTRY

1 cup all-purpose flour

2 tablespoons sugar

½ teaspoon salt

6 tablespoons chilled Kerrygold Irish butter, cut into small pieces

2 large egg yolks

½ teaspoon vanilla extract

1 to 2 tablespoons cold water

FILLING

½ cup raspberry jam

½ cup (1 stick) unsalted Kerrygold Irish butter

1 cup superfine sugar

2 tablespoons grated lemon zest

2 large eggs, beaten

½ cup all-purpose flour, sifted

½ cup ground almonds

Confectioners' sugar for dusting

To make the pastry: Combine the flour, sugar, and salt in a food processor. Pulse 1 to 2 times. Add the butter, a few pieces at a time, and pulse until the mixture resembles coarse crumbs. Add the egg yolks, vanilla, and water, and process until the dough comes together. Turn out the dough onto a work surface, form it into a ball, then wrap it in plastic wrap and refrigerate for 30 minutes.

Preheat the oven to 375°F. Lightly butter two 12-cup mini-muffin pans with 1¾-inch cups. Dust a work surface with flour. Flatten the dough into a disk, cut it in half, then roll out each half to a ¼-inch thickness. With a 2-inch round cookie cutter, cut out 12 rounds of pastry from each half. Put each round in a muffin cup and gently press the dough into the cup.

To make the filling: Put 1 teaspoon of jam into each cup. Combine the butter, superfine sugar, and lemon zest in a food processor and process for 20 to 30 seconds, or until light and fluffy. Beat in the eggs, one at a time. Add the flour and almonds and process 10 to 20 seconds, or until well blended. Spoon the mixture into the pastry-lined cups so that each one is three quarters full.

Bake the tartlets for 25 minutes, or until golden. Remove from the oven and let cool on a wire rack for 10 minutes. Remove the tartlets from the pan and dust with confectioners' sugar.

Oatmeal Cookies

No proper tea would be complete without a selection of cookies, especially classic oatmeal (with or without raisins), shortbreads (page 130), and macaroons (page 132). **Makes about 4½ dozen cookies**

1½ cups all-purpose flour

1 teaspoon baking soda

Pinch of salt

1¼ cups (2½ sticks) unsalted Kerrygold Irish butter at room temperature

½ cup granulated sugar

½ cup packed light brown sugar

1 large egg, beaten

1 teaspoon vanilla extract

3 cups quick-cooking (not instant) Irish oatmeal, such as McCann's brand

¾ cup raisins

½ cup chopped walnuts (optional)

Preheat the oven to 350°F. Line 2 baking sheets with parchment paper.

In a medium bowl, whisk together the flour, baking soda, and salt. In a large bowl, cream the butter and sugars with an electric mixer until light and fluffy. Beat in the egg and vanilla. With a wooden spoon, stir in the flour mixture, oatmeal, raisins, and walnuts, if using. Drop by well-rounded teaspoonfuls onto the prepared sheets, spacing the cookies 2 inches apart.

Bake for 12 to 15 minutes, or until the cookies are golden. Remove from the oven and cool on the baking sheet for 1 minute before transferring to a wire rack to cool completely.

Shortbread Cookies

My mother often made shortbread. Sometimes she baked it in a square pan and cut it into "fingers," and other times she baked it in a round pan and cut it into wedges. Either way, we loved it with a cup of tea or a glass of cold milk. **Serves 8**

½ cup (1 stick) unsalted Kerrygold Irish butter at room temperature

¼ cup superfine sugar

½ cup plus 2 tablespoons cake flour

½ cup cornstarch

Pinch of salt

Preheat the oven to 325°F. Lightly butter an 8-inch round or 8-inch square baking pan.

In a large bowl, cream the butter and sugar with an electric mixer until light and fluffy. In a small bowl, sift together the flour, cornstarch, and salt. Stir the dry ingredients into the butter mixture, one third at a time, mixing until just blended after each addition. Turn out the dough onto a lightly floured work surface, and with floured hands, knead for 1 to 2 minutes, or until smooth.

Press the dough into the prepared pan and prick with a fork in several place to prevent the dough from rising. Bake the shortbread for 18 to 20 minutes, or until the top is pale and the edge is golden. Remove from the oven and let the shortbread cool on a wire rack for 10 to 15 minutes. Cut a square shortbread into 20 to 24 "fingers" or cut the round shortbread into 8 wedges.

Macaroons

Made with ground nuts, chocolate, or flaked coconut, macaroons are one of the world's finest cookies. In Ireland, they frequently appear on a tray of tea cookies. For perfectly shaped macaroons, use a pastry bag; otherwise, drop rounded teaspoons of dough onto a baking pan. **Makes about 30 macaroons**

4 large egg whites

2 cups finely ground toasted almonds or hazelnuts (see Note)

1 cup sugar

Preheat the oven to 325°F. Line 2 baking sheets with parchment paper.

In a large bowl, beat the egg whites with an electric mixer until stiff, glossy peaks form. Gently fold in the nuts and sugar. Fill a pastry bag fitted with a plain nozzle with half of the mixture. Pipe the batter onto each of the prepared baking sheets, leaving 1 1/2 inches between each cookie. They will look somewhat like a Hershey's Kiss.

Bake the macaroons, one pan at a time, for 15 to 20 minutes, or until golden. Remove the pans from the oven and slide the parchment with the cookies onto a work surface. Let the cookies cool completely before removing from the parchment.

NOTE: To toast nuts, spread them out on a baking sheet in a preheated 300°F and toast them for 10 to 15 minutes. Stir once or twice for even toasting.

BUTTERMILK: THE ESSENTIAL INGREDIENT OF IRISH SODA BREAD

Irish playwright George Bernard Shaw loved brown soda bread and once said of it: "Remember that brown bread is a good familiar creature and worth more than his weight in flesh." Unquestionably Ireland's greatest culinary legacy, soda bread—brown, white, and raisin—has been the staff of life for the Irish for centuries and one of the many humble and familiar creature comforts that come to mind when we think of Irish cooking.

Soda bread may be the most cherished of Irish fare, but it's buttermilk, one of its key ingredients, that Irish bakers have used for generations to produce

Castle ruins near Cullahill, County Laois

these hearty loaves of bread. Because buttermilk is naturally high in acid, it reacts well with baking soda or baking powder—both are an alkali—to generate the carbon dioxide that causes batter to rise. It also acts as a natural emulsifier in baking soda bread, dispersing the fat throughout the baked product while its proteins react to sugar and contribute to browning.

Traditionally, loaves of soda bread appear with an "X" cut into the top, either "to let the devil out" as some suggest, or as a symbol of the cross. Originally, soda bread was baked in a cast-iron skillet, but it can be baked free standing on a baking sheet or in a loaf pan. To make a fancier loaf, raisins, dried currants, or caraway seeds are added.

Lemon Curd

Fruit curds flavored with lemon and orange are traditional accompaniments to scones, but they also provide a tangy glaze for fresh berries, a delicious filling for cakes, and a nice flavor to sweetened whipped cream. **Makes about 1¾ cups**

3 large eggs

1 cup sugar

½ cup (1 stick) unsalted Kerrygold Irish butter, cut into small pieces

1 tablespoon finely grated lemon zest

½ cup fresh lemon juice

Combine the eggs and sugar in the top of a double boiler set over simmering water. Whisk together until frothy. Add the butter, lemon zest, and juice. Cook, whisking continuously, for 10 to 15 minutes, or until the mixture thickens and resembles whipped cream. Do not let the mixture boil. Pour the curd into a small bowl or jar, cover, and chill immediately. (It will keep, refrigerated, for 1 week.)

Orange Whiskey Marmalade

Orange marmalade is one of Ireland's most popular preserves, even though it's a gift from a thrifty Scotsman named James Keiller and an eighteenth-century Spanish cargo ship. Legend has it that during a storm a Spanish ship loaded with Seville oranges and apples sought shelter in the Scottish harbor of Dundee. As the storm raged on, the fruit threatened to spoil, so Keiller purchased the bitter oranges and apples, which his wife turned into delicious pots of jam. They were the first batch of Keiller's original Dundee Orange Marmalade, which has since become popular throughout the world. This Irish marmalade, which includes Irish whiskey, is adapted from Folláin, a West Cork producer of preserves, chutneys, and jams, and marmalades. Folláin is the Irish word for "wholesome." Before making the marmalade, prepare the jars, lids, and bands (see Note). **Makes 4 pints**

---

4 large Valencia oranges

2 large or 3 small lemons

2 1/2 cups water

1/8 teaspoon baking soda

One 1 3/4-ounce package powdered fruit pectin

5 1/2 cups sugar

Pinch of ground cloves

1/4 cup Irish whiskey

With a vegetable peeler or zester, remove the zest (the colored part of the peel) in strips from the oranges and lemons and chop. With a knife, scrape off all the white membrane, or pith, from the peeled fruit. Set aside. Chop the fruit, reserving the juice and removing the seeds.

In a large nonreactive saucepan over medium heat, bring the zest, water, and baking soda to a boil. Reduce the heat, cover, and simmer, stirring several times, for 20 minutes, or until the zest begins to soften. Add the fruit, juice, and pectin, and simmer for 20 minutes longer. Stir in the sugar, raise the heat to medium-high, add the cloves, and bring to a boil. Continue to boil, stirring constantly, for 5 to 10 minutes, or until the mixture reaches 220°F on an instant-read thermometer and begins to get syrupy. Stir in the whiskey. Immediately spoon the hot marmalade into the hot sterilized jars, leaving 1/4 inch of headroom at the top of the jars. Wipe the jar rims clean, seal with lids and bands, and store in a cool, dry place for up to 1 year. (Marmalade thickens as it cools, but it may take 2 to 3 days to fully set.)

NOTE: To sterilize jars and lids, wash the jars, lids, and screw bands in hot soapy water, then rinse well. Dry the screw bands. Put the jars and lids in a deep 8-quart pot and add water to cover by 2 inches. Heat the water to nearly boiling, then reduce the heat to low, cover, and keep the jars and lids in the water until ready to use. To process and seal the jars, wipe off the rims with a clean towel. Add the hot marmalade, then firmly screw on the lids with the screw bands. Turn the jars upside-down. After 5 minutes, turn upright. To check the seals, after 12 to 24 hours, press the center of each lid to make sure that it's concave. If the lid springs back, it is not sealed, and the marmalade should be refrigerated and used within a few weeks.

CHAPTER SIX

christmas treats

top: Micro-Mini Christmas Pudding, page 149

bottom: Christmas at Adare Manor, Adare, County Limerick

Traditionally, the biggest and most important festival in the Christian calendar is Christmas, and nowhere is it greeted with more enthusiasm than in Ireland. The spiritual preparation begins with Advent, but the practical preparations begin as early as late October, when Christmas cakes, puddings, and mincemeat begin to fill the pantry and freezer in anticipation of the season.

Alice Taylor, a well-known chronicler of tales of rural Ireland, says that Christmas was always the highlight of the year—"a time of great expectations which climaxed with Christmas Eve and Christmas Day, and then the Wren Day, December 26, (see page 161) brought a burst of color and music into the quiet countryside." In her book *The Night Before Christmas,* she says, "The thought of the variety that Christmas would bring filled us with great anticipation. Lemonade, sweet cake, and chocolates in our home at that time were like manna in the desert."

Christmas is a season that requires, perhaps even demands, tradition. Regardless of how sophisticated Irish cooking has become, there are some classic recipes, especially for Christmas cakes and puddings, that are as treasured as the season itself and that few Irish cooks, or cookbooks, would ever ignore.

Beannachtaí na Féile duit! Season's greetings.

Irish Whiskey Christmas Cake

This is the "Great Irish Cake," the traditional pièce de résistance into which every Irish cook sinks her reputation. Spiced, sweet desserts were highly prized because they included spices and dried fruits that were once difficult and expensive to obtain. You should make this cake at least six weeks ahead and up to two months in advance of serving it. The traditional topping for the cake is a layer of whiskey-flavored marzipan topped with royal icing. Make the marzipan the day before you plan to serve the cake. Serve it with Mulled Wine (page 142), if you like. **Serves 10 to 12**

CAKE

2 cups dried currants

2 cups golden raisins

1 cup dark raisins

2 ounces candied cherries

2 ounces candied mixed citrus peel

Grated zest and juice of 1 lemon

2/3 cup chopped almonds

1½ teaspoons mixed spice (see Note)

½ teaspoon ground nutmeg

1 cup Irish whiskey, plus extra for sprinkling

1 cup (2 sticks) unsalted Kerrygold Irish butter at room temperature

1 cup packed light brown sugar

5 large eggs

2 cups all-purpose flour, sifted

MARZIPAN

2¼ cups blanched almonds, ground in a food processor

1¼ cups superfine sugar

2 large eggs

Drop of vanilla extract

½ teaspoon fresh lemon juice

¼ cup Irish whiskey

2 egg whites, beaten until frothy, for brushing

Sugar for dusting

ROYAL ICING

2 large egg whites

4 cups confectioners' sugar

2 tablespoons fresh lemon juice

To make the cake: The day before baking (and up to 2 months before serving), combine all the dried and candied fruit and peel, the lemon zest and juice, almonds, and spices in a large bowl with ½ cup of the whiskey. Cover and let stand at room temperature overnight.

Preheat the oven to 275°F. Butter a 9-inch round springform pan and line the bottom with a round of parchment or waxed paper. In a large bowl, beat the butter and brown sugar together with an electric mixer until light and fluffy. Add the eggs, one at a time, beating each in

thoroughly and adding some of the sifted flour with each egg. Fold in the remaining flour, and mix in the soaked fruit, one half at a time. Pour the batter into the prepared pan. Bake for 2 to 2½ hours, or until the top is firm to the touch and a skewer inserted into the center comes out clean.

Remove from the oven and let cool in the pan on a wire rack for 30 minutes. Prick the top of the cake with a skewer in several places and pour the remaining ½ cup of whiskey over the top. Run a knife around the inside

(continued)

of the pan and release the sides. Invert the cake onto the rack to cool completely. Remove the lining paper and turn right-side up. Wrap the cake in plastic wrap, then aluminum foil, and store in a cool, dark place to allow the cake to mature. Unwrap the cake every week and sprinkle a few tablespoons of Irish whiskey over the top.

The day before you plan to serve the cake, make the marzipan: In a medium bowl, combine the almonds and superfine sugar. Add the eggs, vanilla, lemon juice, and whiskey, and stir until a smooth paste forms.

Lightly dust a work surface with sugar. Roll the marzipan out to a 10-inch circle. Unwrap the cake and brush the top with the egg whites. Gently lift the marzipan and place it on top of the cake. With a rolling pin, roll it smooth. With a sharp knife, trim the edges so the marzipan fits the top of the cake like a disk. Cover with plastic wrap and refrigerate overnight.

Take the cake out of the refrigerator and make the royal icing: In a large mixing bowl, combine the egg whites, confectioners' sugar, and lemon juice. With an electric mixer, beat for 5 minutes, or until the mixture is stiff enough to spread. With a flexible rubber spatula, spread the icing over the top and sides of the cake.

NOTE: To make mixed spice, combine 1 tablespoon of coriander seeds, 1 crushed cinnamon stick, 1 teaspoon of whole cloves, and 1 teaspoon of allspice berries in a food grinder. Process until finely ground. Add 1 tablespoon of freshly grated nutmeg and 2 teaspoons of ground ginger. Mix thoroughly. Store in an airtight container.

Mulled Wine:

A mulled wine is a cheerful blend of red wine, spices, and a sweetener of sugar, honey, or even maple syrup. Brandy is sometimes added to fortify the fragrant holiday drink, as in this recipe. Hippocrates, the physician from ancient Greece, is credited with inventing the drink, which is called by many names, including mulled or spiced wine, glögg (in Scandinavia), and glühwein (in Germany).

1 bottle dry red wine

½ cup brandy

½ cup Madeira

15 whole cloves

½ cup sugar

5 cinnamon sticks

Grated zest of 1 orange

Grated nutmeg for topping

In a large saucepan over medium heat, combine all the ingredients except the nutmeg. Bring to a boil, then reduce the heat to low and simmer for 5 minutes. Remove from the heat and set aside to let the flavors infuse for up to 4 hours.

To serve, with a slotted spoon, remove the cloves and cinnamon sticks. Ladle the mulled wine into mugs and sprinkle a little nutmeg on top. **Serves 12**

Variation
Mulled Cider: Substitute 3½ cups of cider for the wine.

Traditional Christmas Fruit Cake

Goyas Fine Food, 2-3 Kirwans Lane, in Galway, is a coffee emporium/bakery specializing in handmade confections and wedding cakes. Proprietor Emer Murray has been called "the best baker in Ireland" by the Bridgestone Guide, a well-known guide to fine dining in Ireland. Irresistible sweets such as cranberry-almond tart and blackberry-raspberry roulade draw visitors from all parts of Ireland. Her traditional Christmas cake includes brandy instead of whiskey. She recommends at least 4 weeks of maturing time. **Serves 10 to 12**

3 ¼ cups raisins

3 ¼ cups sultanas

4 ounces candied mixed citrus peel

5 ounces candied cherries

1 cup sliced almonds

Zest and juice of 2 large oranges

Splash of brandy

2 ½ cups all-purpose flour

2 teaspoons ground ginger

2 teaspoons ground cinnamon

2 teaspoons ground nutmeg

1 cup ground almonds

1 cup packed light brown sugar

1 cup (2 sticks) plus 2 tablespoons unsalted Kerrygold Irish butter at room temperature

6 large eggs, beaten

On the night before baking, combine the raisins, sultanas, citrus peel, cherries, almonds, orange zest, and juice in a large bowl. Stir in the brandy, cover, and leave at room temperature for at least 12 hours.

Preheat the oven to 250°F. Butter a 10-inch square pan or a round springform pan and line it with parchment or waxed paper.

In a large bowl, sift together the flour, ginger, cinnamon, and nutmeg. Stir in the ground almonds. Set aside. In another large bowl, beat the sugar and butter with an electric mixer for 3 to 5 minutes, or until light and

fluffy. Beat in the eggs. Stir in the dry ingredients and fold in the fruit mixture. Bake for 2 ½ to 2 ¾ hours, or until a skewer inserted into the center comes out clean. Remove the cake from the oven and let cool completely in the pan on a wire rack. The cake can be covered with marzipan and Royal Icing (page 140) or served plain. It will keep for 6 months wrapped in plastic wrap and aluminum foil and stored in an airtight container.

Christmas Pudding

Often called "plum pudding"—despite the fact that it contains no plums whatsoever—this steamed or boiled pudding was first recorded as "Christmas Pudding" in 1858 in a novel by the British author Anthony Trollope. The name "plum pudding" is probably derived from the use of dried plums as an ingredient in pies and other dishes during medieval times. In the sixteenth and seventeenth centuries, raisins were substituted for the plums, but the dishes retained the term "plum" in their names. In the Victorian era, Christmas plum pudding became a well-loved dessert. Curiously, plum pudding was a latecomer to Ireland, but it caught on quickly and replaced its plainer boiled pudding cousins. To this day it's one of the most traditional of all Christmas dishes. Not to be confused with fruitcake, it's actually more like a dense spice cake. This recipe uses butter rather than the traditional suet. Serve warm with Brandy Hard Sauce or Brandy Cider Sauce (recipes follow).

Serves 10 to 12

³⁄₄ cup dark raisins

½ cup golden raisins

2 ounces candied cherries, halved

2 ounces candied pineapple, chopped

½ cup brandy or dark rum

1¼ cups all-purpose flour

¾ teaspoon baking powder

1 teaspoon grated orange zest

1 teaspoon ground cinnamon

½ teaspoon ground ginger

⅛ teaspoon ground cloves

½ cup packed light brown sugar

4 tablespoons unsalted Kerrygold Irish butter at room temperature

4 large egg whites

⅓ cup pecan halves

2 tablespoons Irish whiskey

Combine the raisins and candied fruit in a glass jar or bowl. Add the brandy, cover, and let stand at room temperature for 3 days.

Butter a 6-cup pudding mold or deep, heat-proof casserole dish. In a medium bowl, whisk together the flour, baking powder, orange zest, cinnamon, ginger, and cloves.

In a large bowl, beat the sugar and butter with an electric mixer until light and fluffy. Add the egg whites and beat well. With a wooden spoon, stir in half of the flour mixture, then half of the soaked fruit mixture. Repeat, stirring in the remaining flour and remaining fruit and brandy. Stir in the pecans. Spoon the batter into the prepared mold, cover with parchment or waxed paper, then cover tightly with foil. Tie the foil in place with string.

Place the mold in a stockpot or Dutch oven fitted with a rack, or place a folded kitchen towel on the bottom of the pot so the bottom of the mold or casserole dish does not come in direct contact with the bottom of the pot. Add enough hot water to the pot to come halfway up the sides of the mold. Cover and steam on medium-low heat for 2 to 2½ hours, or until a skewer inserted into the center comes out clean. (Check the water level once or twice during cooking and add more when necessary.)

Carefully remove the pudding mold from the pot. Remove the foil and parchment, and run a metal spatula around the inside to loosen. Place a serving plate over the mold and invert. Drizzle the whiskey over the top. Slice and serve warm.

Or, if not serving immediately, let the pudding cool, covered, in the mold. When completely cool, unmold, wrap in plastic wrap, then aluminum foil. Refrigerate the pudding for up to 1 week or freeze. To serve, put the pudding back into its mold, cover with parchment or waxed paper and then foil, and steam for 1 hour, as described above, or until heated through. Thaw frozen pudding before reheating.

Brandy Hard Sauce:

This hard sauce and the Brandy Cider Sauce that follows are delicious with Christmas Pudding, Micro-Mini Christmas Puddings (page 149), and Mincemeat Tarts (page 156).

½ cup (1 stick) unsalted Kerrygold Irish butter at room temperature

1½ cups confectioners' sugar, sifted

2 tablespoons brandy

In a small bowl, beat the butter and sugar together with an electric mixer until light and fluffy. Add the brandy and beat until smooth. Transfer to a small bowl or crock, cover, and refrigerate for up to 2 days. Return to room temperature before serving. **Makes ¾ cup**

Brandy Cider Sauce:

½ cup apple cider

¼ cup packed light brown sugar

1 tablespoon cornstarch

2 tablespoons brandy

1 teaspoon unsalted Kerrygold Irish butter at room temperature

In a small saucepan over medium heat, whisk together the cider, sugar, and cornstarch. Bring to a boil, whisking constantly, and cook for 2 minutes, or until the mixture thickens. Stir in the brandy and butter. Remove from the heat and let cool. Transfer to a small bowl or crock, cover, and refrigerate for up to 2 days. Return to room temperature before serving. **Makes ¾ cup**

Bantry House Guinness Cake

Overlooking Bantry Bay in scenic County Cork, Bantry House boasts one of the most spectacular settings in all of Ireland. Formerly the seat of the Earls of Bantry, the antiques-filled house has been owned by the White family since 1739. The second Earl of Bantry, who was mainly responsible for collecting the furniture, paintings, and objets d'art that fill the home, is also credited with laying out the formal gardens. This Guinness Cake is regularly served at tea, although it is a favorite at Christmas as an alternative to the traditional whiskey cake since it can be baked and served immediately. Bantry House is a member of the Hidden Ireland (see page 29). **Serves 8 to 10**

1 cup (2 sticks) unsalted Kerrygold Irish butter, cut into pieces

1¼ cups Guinness Stout

1 cup packed light brown sugar

3½ cups mixed raisins and sultanas

4 ounces candied mixed citrus peel

4 cups self-rising flour

2 teaspoons mixed spice (see Note, page 142)

4 ounces candied cherries

3 large eggs, beaten

Preheat the oven to 325°F. Butter an 8-inch square cake pan and line it with parchment or waxed paper.

In a medium saucepan over medium heat, combine the butter, Guinness, sugar, raisins and sultanas, and citrus peel. Bring gently to a boil and cook, stirring frequently, for 3 to 4 minutes, or until slightly thickened. Remove from the heat and let cool for 10 to 15 minutes.

In a large bowl, sift together the flour and mixed spice. Stir in the raisin and stout mixture and the cherries. Add the eggs and stir until well blended. Spoon the batter into the prepared pan and smooth the top.

Bake the cake on the middle shelf of the oven for 60 to 70 minutes, or until a skewer inserted into the center comes out clean. Remove from the oven and let the cake cool in the pan on a wire rack for 30 minutes. Invert the cake onto the rack to cool completely. Remove the lining paper and turn the cake right side up. Serve immediately, or wrap the cake in plastic wrap, then aluminum foil, and store in a cool, dark place for 2 to 3 weeks to allow the cake to mature.

MAIRGEAD MOR, "BIG FAIR DAY"

Over most of Western Europe, particularly in those areas connected with the ancient Celts, December 8 was associated with the celebration of the festival of the winter solstice.

In Ireland, December 8 is also celebrated as *Mairgead Mor,* or the "Big Fair Day." Brian Nolan, a Loughrea, County Galway native, remembers it as a day of great celebration, when farmers would converge on town to sell their crops, livestock, and poultry, and women would come with them to spend their "butter and egg money" on holiday gifts and goodies.

According to Nolan, "*Mairgead Mor* was an amazing sight to me as a child in the early 60s before marts and supermarkets modernised everything. On that day, everyone came to town—the ruddy-faced, wool-capped men with their sturdy womenfolk; the too-thin gaggles of wide-eyed children—on horses, in donkey and cart, on bicycles, and on foot, and everyone carried something for the fair. They arrived before dawn, and left, mess of straw and leavings behind them, after dark.

"Geese by the hundred, turkeys and chickens by the thousand, all 'live,' tied to the back of upturned donkey carts between loads of turf. Mounds of potato sacks brimmed with Kerrs Pinks and Banners from Clare; huge heads of cabbage and turnips; bunches of parsnip and carrots, and the very rare bushel of brussels sprouts. Wheels of hardy cheddar, and what seemed like acres of flats of eggs in hues of brown and white, with the bigger duck-eggs, bluish in the winter sunlight.

"The fowl would be raucous, hog-tied or closeted in bushel baskets with their heads poking out, or in more modern times, poking their heads out of car-boots, and all cackling and clucking and gobbling away to their hearts' content. The 'townies' and some city market buyers made their canny way, back and forth between the rows of sellers, examining here, feeling there, commenting on the size and weight, and what they were fed on, and whether they were spring or summer birds.

"Amid all that was the excitement of the shops, the bustle of the women going in to settle their account with the harvest, butter, and turkey money enabling them to pay off the tab and get some new clothes for themselves and the children, now wide-eyed in expectation and appreciation of the beautiful goods and sweet chocolates they were able to see and touch now."

December 8 was one of the most important dates in the Celtic calendar as it marked the celebration of a farmer's success and the approach of the New Year. In modern Ireland, it's the biggest shopping day of the year.

Micro-Mini Christmas Puddings

"Cover the kettle and simmer the pudding over low heat for 3 hours, or until firm." If these directions are enough to make you think twice about making a pudding for the holidays, then you'll love this recipe for individual puddings that you "steam" in the microwave. I have to admit my own reluctance to resort to microwave cooking for a holiday as sacred as Christmas, but once I tasted these puddings, I was won over. As you can see from the list of ingredients, the only shortcut here is in the baking, and when you use deep, microwave-safe teacups or 8-ounce ramekins, the cooked puddings even have the shape of one cooked in a traditional pudding mold. Serve with Rum Butter with Ginger Chips or Baileys Irish Cream Butter (page 158). **Serves 8**

2 cups raisins

2 cups golden raisins

4 ounces candied mixed citrus peel

2 ounces candied cherries, chopped

½ cup chopped walnuts

Grated zest and juice of 1 lemon

1 Granny Smith apple, peeled, cored, and grated

1 cup all-purpose flour

Pinch of salt

1 teaspoon mixed spice (see Note, page 142)

½ teaspoon cinnamon

¼ teaspoon nutmeg

¾ cup fresh white bread crumbs (see Note, page 19)

¼ cup brown sugar

4 tablespoons unsalted Kerrygold Irish butter, melted

2 large eggs, beaten

2 tablespoons molasses

1½ cups Guinness Stout

2 tablespoons rum

The day before baking, combine the dried and candied fruit, walnuts, lemon zest and juice, and apple in a large bowl. Mix well. In a small bowl, sift together the flour, salt, and spices and stir into the fruit. Stir in the bread crumbs and sugar and mix again. In another small bowl, combine the butter, eggs, molasses, Guinness, and rum. Pour this into the dry ingredients and stir to blend. Cover and refrigerate overnight.

Butter 8 microwave-safe teacups or eight 8-ounce ramekins and line with a piece of plastic wrap long enough to cover the top. Divide the mixture into the cups and push the batter down with a spoon. Arrange the puddings in a circle in a microwave oven. Cook on defrost (power level 3) for 20 minutes, then cook on high (power level 10) for 10 minutes, or until a skewer inserted into the center comes out clean. Remove from the oven and let cool on a wire rack for 10 minutes. Uncover, invert the cups onto dessert plates, remove the plastic wrap, and serve warm.

Christmas Pudding Ice Cream

This ice cream pudding is a delicious, lighter alternative to traditional Christmas puddings like the two preceding recipes. It uses the same fruits, soaked overnight in port, but instead of being baked, the pudding is frozen like ice cream. Any combination of chopped dried fruits (golden raisins, figs, cranberries, apricots, dates) can be used, but be sure to include candied red and green cherries or dried cranberries for a colorful look. **Serves 6 to 8**

1 pound dried mixed fruit, chopped

Port for soaking

¼ cup sugar

⅔ cup water

4 large egg yolks

2 cups heavy (whipping) cream

1 teaspoon vanilla extract

1 cup almonds, toasted (see Note, page 132)

The day before making the ice cream, combine the dried fruit in a glass bowl and pour in enough port to cover. Cover and let soak overnight at room temperature. Drain before continuing with the recipe.

In a saucepan over medium heat, combine the sugar and water and bring to a gentle boil. Cook for 4 to 6 minutes, or until the sugar dissolves and begins to get syrupy.

In a medium bowl, beat the egg yolks with an electric mixer until light and fluffy. Slowly stir the syrup into the yolks. Beat until the mixture thickens to a mousse-like consistency.

In a small bowl, whip the cream with an electric mixer until soft peaks form. Fold the whipped cream and then the vanilla into the mousse. Fold in the soaked and drained fruit and the almonds. Pour the mixture into a 5- or 6-cup pudding mold or metal bowl, cover with plastic wrap, and freeze until firm, preferably overnight.

To serve, dip the mold or bowl into warm water to loosen, then invert onto a serving plate. Using a knife that's been dipped into hot water, cut the pudding into slices.

LEGEND OF THE CHRISTMAS CANDLE

Many Irish traditions stem from Celtic mythology and Christian rituals. The tradition of feasting on Christmas Day marks the end of Advent, a four-week period of fasting in the Christian calendar. The Christmas cakes, fruit cakes, and special breads savored on that day have always held a special place in the Celtic household. Mince pies and plum puddings were symbols of a fertile and rich reserve from which new energy would emerge.

Christmas is also a season of family celebrations, and the tradition of the Christmas candle is one that has been handed down from generation to generation. As Alice Taylor reports in her book *The Night Before Christmas,* "the lighting of the Christmas candle marked the transition from day into night on Christmas Eve. It was the light of Christmas and the key that opened the door into the holy night."

A tall, thick candle is placed on the sill of the most prominent window in the home. On Christmas Eve, the youngest child usually lights the candle, which stands as a welcoming light for neighbors and holiday visitors, travelers like Mary and Joseph, who searched for shelter and warmth.

The Mills Inn, Ballyvourney,
County Cork

Mother's White Fruitcake

This recipe is one my mother simply called "white fruitcake." When we were children, we didn't appreciate the flavor and texture of a traditional Irish Christmas cake, so she adapted this recipe from one she found in the Boston Globe's "Confidential Chat." Because it doesn't involve soaking any of the fruit in dark spirits like whiskey, rum, Guinness, or brandy, it was always more appealing to us when we were kids. We also loved the whole red and green cherries. **Serves 10 to 12**

6 ounces whole candied red cherries

6 ounces whole candied green cherries

1 cup golden raisins

6 ounces candied pineapple

1 cup chopped walnuts

2 cups all-purpose flour

½ teaspoon baking soda

¼ teaspoon salt

¼ teaspoon ground allspice

¾ cup (1½ sticks) unsalted Kerrygold Irish butter at room temperature

1 cup sugar

5 large eggs

Preheat the oven to 300°F. Butter a 10-inch tube or bundt pan. Dust with flour and tap out excess.

In a medium bowl, combine the cherries, raisins, pineapple, and walnuts. Stir in ¼ cup of the flour. Set aside.

In a medium bowl, sift together the remaining 1¾ cups of the flour with the baking soda, salt, and allspice. In a large bowl, beat the butter and sugar together with an electric mixer until light and fluffy. Add the eggs, one at a time, beating well and scraping the bowl after each addition. Add the flour mixture and then stir in the fruit mixture. Spoon the batter into the prepared pan.

Bake the cake for 60 to 75 minutes, or until a skewer inserted into the center comes out clean. Remove from the oven and let cool in the pan for 10 minutes. Invert the pan onto a wire rack and let cool completely.

Slice and serve immediately, or wrap in plastic wrap, then in aluminum foil, and refrigerate for up to 1 week.

Bushmills Boiled Fruitcake

This version of an Irish Christmas cake is an interesting one because the dried and candied fruits are cooked with butter, brown sugar, and pineapple juice before they're mixed with batter. This technique, along with the addition of crushed pineapple, makes the cake exceptionally moist. The recipe was given to me nearly a decade ago by the chef at the Hillside Restaurant in Hillsborough, County Down, and it's become a family favorite. Unlike other fruitcakes, it doesn't need to mature and it's especially nice for gift giving when baked in small loaf pans. **Makes 1 large or 4 to 5 small loaves**

One 20-ounce can crushed pineapple, undrained

½ cup (1 stick) unsalted Kerrygold Irish butter

½ cup light brown sugar

2 cups golden raisins

4 ounces candied cherries

4 ounces candied mixed peel

1 cup self-rising flour

1 cup all-purpose flour

1 teaspoon baking soda

1 teaspoon mixed spice (see Note, page 142)

2 large eggs, beaten

2 to 3 tablespoons Irish whiskey

In a large saucepan over medium heat, combine the pineapple, butter, sugar, raisins, cherries, and zest. Bring to a boil and continue boiling, stirring constantly, for 5 minutes. Remove from the heat and let cool completely.

Preheat the oven to 325°F. Butter a 9-x-5-x-3-inch loaf pan or four to five 3-x-2-x-1½-inch mini-loaf pans.

In a large bowl, whisk together the flours, soda, and mixed spice. Stir in the eggs. Add this to the fruit mixture, and with a wooden spoon, blend thoroughly. Spoon the batter into the pan(s) and smooth the top with a wet spatula. Bake the cake for 60 to 75 minutes (test with a skewer after 60 minutes), or bake the mini-loaves for about 55 minutes (test with a skewer

after 45 minutes). Remove from the oven and let cool in the pan on a wire rack. Prick the top in several places with a skewer, and drizzle with the whiskey while the cake is still warm.

Remove cake from pan and let cool completely on a wire rack. Wrap in plastic wrap, then in aluminum foil. (For those who like the idea of administering a daily dose of spirits, unwrap and redrizzle at your own discretion.) The cakes can be kept at room temperature for several days, or in the refrigerator for up to 1 week. They can be frozen for 1 to 2 months.

Cinnamon Berry Christmas Bread

This rather unusual Christmas bread is one that Dingle-born Eleanor Walsh, head chef at Dublin's Eden restaurant, has enjoyed since she was a kid, "especially after a restorative Christmas morning swim!" she adds. The bread is simple to make and can be prepared in advance, so it's suitable to follow whatever Christmas traditions your family enjoys. **Serves 8 to 10**

2 cups all-purpose flour

1 teaspoon baking powder

½ teaspoon ground cinnamon

8 ounces mixed fresh or frozen and thawed berries (strawberries, blueberries, raspberries)

1 cup sugar

2 large eggs, beaten

3 tablespoons Crème Fraîche (page 24)

Preheat the oven to 375°F. Butter a 9-x-5-x-3-inch loaf pan and dust with flour. Tap out the excess.

In a small mixing bowl, sift together the flour, baking powder, and cinnamon. In a large mixing bowl, mash the berries to a rough purée with a fork or vegetable masher. Add the sugar and mix well. Whisk in the eggs. Add the flour mixture and stir until well blended. Stir in the crème fraîche. Spoon the batter into the prepared pan.

Bake the bread for 70 to 75 minutes, or until a skewer inserted into the top comes out clean. Remove from the oven and let cool in the pan on a wire rack for 15 minutes before slicing. Serve spread with butter.

Mincemeat Tarts

Mincemeat is one of the oldest pie fillings and was esteemed as holiday fare in the era of Henry VII (1457–1509), who proclaimed Christmas a day of feasting in England. Back in the days of ancient Rome, mincemeat made its first appearance when Apicium, a Roman chef who wrote the first known cookbook, preserved meat with honey to retard the growth of bacteria. Later, other cooks found that meat could be kept for a number of months if it were mixed with fruit, spices, and sugar. Some early recipes for mincemeat were made with veal or mutton, and gradually cooks added ingredients like apples, Seville oranges, and even red wine. In Elizabethan England, huge mince pies were made during the twelve days of Christmas, and it became customary to offer a visiting guest a slice. The leap from England to Ireland was a short one, so mincemeat became a favorite ingredient in an Irish Christmas as well, especially in the form of these miniature mince pies. When there was no longer any need to preserve meat with honey or spices, the meat in mincemeat was eliminated and replaced with fruit alone, although some cooks still use a bit of suet in their recipes. Serve these little pies warm with Rum Butter with Ginger Chips (page 158) or Baileys Irish Cream Butter (page 158). **Makes 12 tartlets**

CRUST

1 3/4 cups all-purpose flour

1/3 cup confectioners' sugar

1/2 teaspoon salt

2 teaspoons grated orange zest

1/2 cup (1 stick) cold unsalted Kerrygold Irish butter, cut into pieces

1 large egg yolk

3 tablespoons orange juice

FILLING

1/3 cup confectioners' sugar

3/4 cup prepared mincemeat (see Note)

3 tablespoons chopped walnuts

1 teaspoon grated orange zest

1/2 teaspoon ground cinnamon

1 egg beaten with 1 tablespoon water

To make the crust: Sift the flour into the bowl of a food processor. Add the sugar, salt, orange zest, and butter. Pulse 5 to 10 times, or until the mixture resembles coarse crumbs. In a small bowl, whisk together the egg yolk and orange juice. Add to the flour mixture and process for 10 to 20 seconds, or until the dough comes together. Dust a work surface with flour. Turn out the dough,

form it into a ball, then flatten into a disk. Cut in half, cover with waxed paper, and refrigerate for 30 minutes.

Preheat the oven to 375°F. Butter a 12-cup tartlet pan or a mini-muffin pan with 2 1/2-inch cups.

Dust a work surface with flour. Roll out half of the dough to a 1/4-inch-thick round. With a 3-inch cookie

(continued)

Mincemeat Tarts (continued)

cutter, cut out 12 rounds of pastry. Put a round in each tartlet cup and gently press in the dough, leaving a slight overhang.

To make the filling: In a small bowl, combine the confectioners' sugar, mincemeat, walnuts, orange zest, and cinnamon. Divide the mixture among the crusts. Roll out the remaining dough and with a 3-inch cookie cutter, cut out 12 more rounds. Place the rounds on top of the mincemeat. With a fork, press the edges of the top and bottom crusts together. Brush the pastry with the egg wash. Cut a small "X" in the center of each pie to vent steam.

Bake the tartlets for 30 to 35 minutes, or until golden. Remove from the oven and transfer to a wire rack and let cool in the pan for 5 to 7 minutes. Remove the tarts from the pan and serve warm with one of the hard sauces, or cool completely and store in an airtight container for up to 3 days.

NOTE: Prepared mincemeat is available readymade in jars or condensed in boxes. If using condensed, reconstitute with 2/3 cup of water.

Rum Butter with Ginger Chips:
Somewhat like hard sauce, this rum butter and the Baileys Irish Cream Butter that follows can also be served with Christmas puddings and mincemeat desserts.

1 cup (2 sticks) unsalted Kerrygold Irish butter at room temperature

3/4 cup packed light brown sugar

1/2 teaspoon ground nutmeg

3 tablespoons dark rum

1/4 cup crystallized ginger chips

1/2 teaspoon grated lemon zest

In a medium bowl, beat the butter with an electric mixer until light and fluffy. Beat in the sugar and nutmeg until smooth. Stir in the rum, ginger chips, and lemon zest. Transfer to a small bowl or crock, cover, and refrigerate for up to 3 days. Return to room temperature before serving. **Makes 2 cups**

Baileys Irish Cream Butter:

3/4 cup unsalted Kerrygold Irish butter

3/4 cup confectioners' sugar, sifted

2 to 3 tablespoons Baileys Irish Cream

In a medium bowl, beat the butter and sugar together with an electric mixer until light and fluffy. Add the Baileys, one tablespoon at a time, and beat until smooth. Transfer to a small bowl or crock, cover, and refrigerate for up to 3 days. Return to room temperature before serving. **Makes 1 1/2 cups**

Royal Apple Pies

Con Traas, a delightful transplanted Dutchman, operates the Apple Farm, a fruit-growing paradise in Moorstown, County Tipperary (see page 76). In addition to growing several varieties of apples, he also provides recipes for his produce in a quarterly newsletter. He offered this recipe for Royal Apple Pies, which he says "dates from medieval times, although at that time real meat would have been used in place of the more common fruit and spiced mixture most cooks use today." Like other mincemeat desserts, these are traditionally associated with Christmas. **Makes 12 tartlets**

CRUST	FILLING	TOPPING
1¼ cups all-purpose flour	4 Granny Smith apples, peeled, cored, and grated	2 egg whites
⅓ cup confectioners' sugar	¾ cup prepared mincemeat (see Note, page 158)	¼ cup superfine sugar
Pinch of salt	3 tablespoons sugar	
⅔ cup (about 1¼ sticks) cold unsalted Kerrygold Irish butter, cut into pieces	Pinch of mixed spice (see Note, page 142)	
2 large egg yolks		
1 tablespoon water		

To make the crust: Sift the flour into the bowl of a food processor. Add the confectioners' sugar, salt, and butter. Pulse 5 to 10 times, or until the mixture resembles coarse crumbs. Whisk together the egg yolks and water, add to the flour mixture, and process for 10 to 20 seconds, or until the dough comes together. Dust a work surface with flour. Turn out the dough, form it into a ball, then flatten into a disk. Cut the dough in half, cover with waxed paper, and refrigerate for 30 minutes.

Preheat the oven to 400°F. Butter a 12-cup tartlet pan or mini-muffin pan with 2½-inch cups.

Dust a work surface with flour. Roll out half of the dough to a ¼-inch-thick round. With a 3-inch cookie cutter, cut out 6 rounds. Put a round in each tartlet cup and gently press in the dough. Repeat with the second half of the dough. Bake the tartlet shells for 14 to 16 minutes, or until lightly browned. Maintain the oven temperature.

To make the filling: In a large bowl, combine the apples, mincemeat, sugar and mixed spice. Spoon into the tartlet shells. Bake for 20 to 25 minutes, or until the mixture is bubbling.

To make the topping: In a medium bowl, beat the egg whites with an electric mixer until soft peaks form. Add the sugar and beat until stiff peaks form. Spread the meringue mixture over the filled tartlets and bake for 10 to 12 minutes longer, or until the meringue is lightly browned.

Shortbread Mince Pies

Griffin's Bakery, on Shop Street, in Galway, is well-known for its luscious Christmas confections. One of Jimmy Griffin's specialties is homemade whiskey mincemeat, which he uses in his shortbread pies. The mince pies are actually individual shortbread cookies, which he fills with mincemeat, then dusts with confectioners' sugar. He suggests serving them warm with whipped cream and mulled wine, but these little pies can also be stored in an airtight container for up to a week. This recipe, a variation of Griffin's, is made with prepared mincemeat spiked with a couple of tablespoons of Irish whiskey. Serve with Brandy Hard Sauce (page 145) and Mulled Wine (page 142). **Makes 18 to 20 pies**

1⅓ cups prepared mincemeat (see Note, page 158)

2 tablespoons Irish whiskey

3 cups all-purpose flour

½ cup granulated sugar

1 cup (2 sticks) cold unsalted Kerrygold Irish butter, cut into small pieces

1 large egg yolk

⅓ to ½ cup ice water

Confectioners' sugar for dusting

In a small bowl, combine the mincemeat and whiskey and set aside. Combine the flour, granulated sugar, and butter in a food processor. Pulse 8 to 10 times, or until the mixture resembles coarse crumbs. Whisk together the egg yolk and ⅓ cup of the water. Add it to the dry ingredients and process for 10 to 20 seconds, or until the dough comes together. If necessary, add the rest of the water. Gather the dough and press it together until it forms a ball. Cover with plastic wrap and refrigerate for 1 hour.

Preheat the oven to 325°F. Line a baking sheet with parchment paper.

Cut the dough in half. Dust a work surface with flour. Roll out half the dough to a ¼-inch thickness. With a 3-inch pastry cutter, cut out 18 to 20 rounds. Place half the rounds on the prepared baking sheet, spacing them 1 inch apart. Put 1 teaspoon of mincemeat in the center of each, then cover with a plain pastry round. With a fork, press the edges to seal and brush with a little water. Pierce the tops with a fork.

Bake the pies for 25 to 27 minutes, or until lightly browned. Transfer the pies to a wire rack to cool. Roll out and fill the remaining half of the dough, then gather the scraps, reroll, and make additional pies. Dust the cooled pies with confectioners' sugar. Serve immediately, or store in an airtight container for up to 3 days.

HUNTING OF THE WREN

One of the richest traditions the Irish observe at Christmas time is the age-old custom of "Hunting the Wren," an event that takes place on St. Stephen's Day, December 26. The festival commemorates an ancient ritual of rural revelers, who would travel from door to door begging for money or treats. The participants, originally called Wren Boys or mummers, often carried a wren in a cage and pretended that the bird was asking for alms. More popular, however, was the tradition of carrying a stuffed wren hung on a pole or placed in a bed of evergreens or furze, a spiny shrub. As they walked around the village, they sang: "The wren, the wren, the king of all birds, St. Stephen's day was caught in the furze; Up with kattle and down with the pan, Give us our hansel [money] to bury the wren."

The Wren Boys came masked and dressed in outlandish costumes, often made of straw. They would visit houses in rural neighborhoods, playing accordions and drums called *bodhráns* (pronounced bowrawn) and begging for donations for the evening's Wren dance. Tradition has it that the first group of Wren Boys would be welcomed to a house because they were said to bring good luck, but those who came afterwards were usually not as well appreciated. At the end of the day, it was customary to bury the wren, so if the boys weren't suitably rewarded at a particular household, they retaliated by burying the wren opposite the front door to prevent luck from entering the house for that year.

Although this tradition has died out in many parts of Ireland, it is very much alive and well in Dingle, in County Kerry. In his book *Green and Gold: The Wrenboys of Dingle,* local author Steve MacDonogh says, "The Wren is an explosion of light, color, and boisterous exuberance in the midst of winter's gloom, and has continued as an unbroken tradition—changing, but never dying out." The great tradition in Dingle is quite competitive, with Wren Boys vying for bragging rights for "best turn-out," "best music," and "best rigs." Other popular St. Stephen's Day activities in Ireland include going to the races or joining a local fox hunt.

Wren Boys Celebrate in Dingle, County Kerry
(Photo courtesy of Bernie Coogin)

Glossary

Baileys Irish Cream

Made from Irish whiskey, double cream, neutral spirits, and natural flavors, Baileys Irish Cream was the first of several cream liqueurs produced in Ireland.

Cashel Blue cheese

Produced by Jane and Louis Grubb in Fethard, County Tipperary, Cashel Blue has been made from the milk of pedigreed Friesian cows since 1986. It is best eaten at around four months old, when it turns a rich yellow and develops a buttery flavor. Cashel is Ireland's best-known blue cheese.

Celtic Crossing Liqueur

Made from a secret recipe from deep within the heart of Ireland, Celtic Crossing liqueur is a blend of Irish spirits, cognac, and a hint of honey. It was named for those emigrants who set out on their own "Celtic Crossing" years ago, and it celebrates the migration of Irish culture to the four corners of the world.

Coulis

A general term for a thick purée or sauce, often made of fruit, especially berries.

Cranachan

A soft, sweet honey, cream, and oatmeal dessert.

Digestive biscuits

Semisweet crackers often served with tea. Carr's brand Wheatalo Biscuits make a good base of crumbs for cheesecake.

Flummery

A soft, sweet pudding made of stewed fruit, thickened with cornstarch or oatmeal and sweetened with honey or sugar.

Irish Mist Liqueur

Made from distilled spirits, honey, and herbs, Irish Mist is a popular liqueur for drinking and a flavorful ingredient in cooking. It was Ireland's first liqueur.

Irish whiskey marmalade

A preserve made with thickly sliced oranges and flavored with Irish whiskey. Folláin, Morleys, Alexander's, Chivers, and Fruitfield are some popular brands.

Mead

Once the drink of the ancient Gauls and Anglo-Saxons, who made it from fermented honey and water, today mead is made in Bunratty, in County Clare, from white wine, honey, and herbs. Known as Bunratty Meade, it is served as a welcoming drink at the famous medieval castle banquets, but many Irish chefs use it in sauces and desserts.

Oatmeal

One of Ireland's most important cereal crops, oatmeal is used in breads, biscuits, and cakes and also in crusts and toppings. Steel-cut, or pinhead, oats are whole-grain groats (the inner portion of the oat kernel) that have been cut into two or three pieces. Minimal processing helps steel-cut oats to retain their distinctive taste and nutritional value. They're best when you toast them first to bring out their nutty flavor. Flahavan's, Odlums, Whites Speedicook, and McCann's are the most popular brands. McCann's is the most widely available in the United States.

Pinhead oats. *See* Oatmeal

Poitín

Distilled from barley, sugar, and water, *poitín* was originally made in pot stills over a peat fire. It was banned in Ireland in 1661 and only recently was legalized. Bunratty Poitín (also known as "potcheen") is now sold throughout the country as well as in the United States. *Poitín* is sometimes used as a substitute for Irish whiskey.

Porter. *See* Stout

Posset

Originally a drink made with milk, wine, or ale, a posset is now served as a chilled, cream-enriched dessert.

Steel-cut oats. *See* Oatmeal

Stout

A strong, dark beer made with hops and dark-roasted barley. Guinness and Murphy's are Ireland's most popular stouts. Originally called porter, Arthur Guinness renamed the beer stout for its strong, bold taste.

Syllabub

Originally a thick, frothy drink, a syllabub is now served as a chilled, cream-enriched dessert, usually flavored with lemon, brandy, wine, or whiskey.

Whiskey, Irish

Irish whiskey undergoes a triple distillation process and a three-year maturation period that distinguish its flavor from that of Scotch whisky. The oldest whiskey brands are those of the Irish Distillers Group: Jameson, Bushmills, Paddy, Midleton, and John Powers. The newest brands are Locke's, Tyrconnell, and Kilbeggan, from the reopened Cooley-John Locke's

Distillery, in Kilbeggan, County Westmeath; and Knappogue Single Malt, named Spirit of the Year in 1999 by *Food & Wine* magazine. Single malts are unblended whiskeys produced in a single distillery from malted barley (the malting occurs when the barley is spread out on a warm floor and allowed to germinate, or sprout, before being dried).

Resources

Use this guide to find food and beverages from Ireland, ingredients called for in some recipes, and growers and producers mentioned in this book.

To find an Irish shop in your area where some of these products are available, contact Enterprise Ireland, 345 Park Avenue, New York, NY 10154; phone 212-371-3600. Or try the Irish Food Board (*An Bord Bia*), 400 North Michigan Avenue, Chicago, IL 60611; phone 773-871-6749. Visit them online at www.bordbia.ie.

For information on travel to Ireland, including accommodations, culture, sports, and festivals, contact Tourism Ireland, 345 Park Avenue, New York, NY 10154; phone 800-223-6470. Visit them online at www.tourismireland.com.

Apples

The Apple Farm, a fruit farm specializing in apples, pears, raspberries, and strawberries, also produces a range of premium, natural apple beverages. In Ireland, visit the Apple Farm in Moorstown, Cahir, County Tipperary. Visit them online at www.theapplefarm.com.

Biscuit, Candy, Cookies, Crackers, Honey, Marmalades, Preserves, and Tea

To mail order these items, or request a catalog, contact the following: Bewley Irish Imports, phone 800-BEWLEY, www.bewleyirishimports.com; Traditional Irish Foods, phone 800-877-IRELAND, www.foodireland.com; Celtic Brands, phone 888-894-7474, www.celticbrands.com.

Blueberries

Derryvilla Farm, a twenty-acre blueberry plantation in Derryvilla, near Portarlington, in County Offaly, is slowly reviving and enhancing the original home of the fraughan, or blueberry, in Ireland. Visit them online at www.derryvillabluberries.com.

Butter

Kerrygold is the international trademark of the Irish Dairy Board (*An Bord Bainne*). To find out which supermarkets sell Kerrygold Irish butter, contact the Irish Dairy Board, 825 Green Bay Road, Suite 200, Wilmette, IL 60091; phone 847-256-8289. Or visit them online at www.idbusa.com. To mail order Kerrygold butter, phone Traditional Irish Foods, 800-877-IRELAND. Or visit them online at www.foodireland.com.

Celtic Crossing Liqueur

To find out where you can buy Celtic Crossing, phone Great Spirits, 800-882-8140, or visit them online at www.greatspirits.com.

Hidden Ireland

For information on the Hidden Ireland, which offers accommodations in country homes and estates, visit them online at www.hiddenireland.com.

Irish Mist and Tullamore Dew

In Ireland, visit the Tullamore Dew Heritage Center, Bury Quay, in Tullamore, County Offaly, for a tour, tasting, and history of Tullamore Dew and Irish Mist. Or visit them online at www.tullamore-dew.org.

Marzipan

Odense marzipan and almond paste, products of Denmark, are available in most supermarkets. To find a location near you, phone Andre Prost, Inc., 800-243-0897, or visit them online at www.andreprost.com.

Mead and Poitín

To find out where you can buy authentic Irish mead (bottled as Bunratty Meade) and *poitín* (bottled as Bunratty Potcheen), phone Camelot Importing Co., 800-4-CAMELOT.

Mincemeat

Several Irish companies make mincemeat, including Folláin, in Ballyvourney, County Cork; however, they are not generally available in the United States. None Such Mincemeat, a product of Eagle Family Foods, is widely available in jars and condensed in boxes. Visit them at www.eaglenonesuch.com.

Oatmeal

McCann's brand Irish oatmeal (quick-cooking, instant, and steel-cut) is available in most supermarkets. McCann's, Flahavan's, and Odlums brands are available from Traditional Irish Foods, phone 800-877-IRELAND, www.foodireland.com; and from Celtic Brands, phone 888-894-7474, www.celticbrands.com.

Whiskey

In Ireland, there are five whiskey museum/visitor centers that provide tours and tastings. Three are owned by Pernod Ricard/Irish Distillers: the Old Jameson Distillery, Bow Street, Dublin 7; the Jameson Heritage Center, Midleton, County Cork; and the Old Bushmills Distillery, 2 Distillery Road, Bushmills, County Antrim. For online information visit www.irishdistillers.ie, or www.whiskeytours.ie; the other two are Tullamore Dew Heritage Center, Bury Quay, Tullamore, County Offaly (www.tullamore-dew.org); Locke's Distillery Museum, Kilbeggan, County Westmeath (www.lockeswhiskeymuseum.ie).

Index

Index

Table of Equivalents

The exact equivalents in the following tables have been rounded for convenience.

Liquid/Dry Measures

U.S.	Metric
¼ teaspoon	1.25 milliliters
½ teaspoon	2.5 milliliters
1 teaspoon	5 milliliters
1 tablespoon (3 teaspoons)	15 milliliters
1 fluid ounce (2 tablespoons)	30 milliliters
¼ cup	60 milliliters
⅓ cup	80 milliliters
½ cup	120 milliliters
1 cup	240 milliliters
1 pint (2 cups)	480 milliliters
1 quart (4 cups, 32 ounces)	960 milliliters
1 gallon (4 quarts)	3.84 liters
1 ounce (by weight)	28 grams
1 pound	454 grams
2.2 pounds	1 kilogram

Length

U.S.	Metric
⅛ inch	3 millimeters
¼ inch	6 millimeters
½ inch	12 millimeters
1 inch	2.5 centimeters

Oven Temperature

Fahrenheit	Celsius	Gas
250	120	½
275	140	1
300	150	2
325	160	3
350	180	4
375	190	5
400	200	6
425	220	7
450	230	8
475	240	9
500	260	10